The Vital Parenting Skills and Happy Children

A 5 Full-Length Parenting Book Compilation for Raising Happy Kids Who Are Honest, Respectful and Well-Adjusted

Frank Dixon

Book Description

Does your kid always run to their room when scolded, throws a tantrum in the middle of the road, uses abusive language, and misbehaves with their peers and elders? Or do they seem scared to take on new challenges because the fear of failure and loss is too much to handle? Are they not mentally strong to regulate their emotions and behaviors? Do they show reluctance to try things they aren't comfortable with? Are you afraid the outside world will break their confidence and manipulate them?

If so, then this is the book you need to read right now!

Often kids, young and old, fear trying new things for the sole reason of being hurt. And as parents, we only do more harm by trying to keep them clutched instead of motivating and encouraging them to go for it. Instead, we should be the ones to offer them opportunities for growth and development, so they learn not to be bullied by their inner voices that keep putting them down.

In *How Parents Can Raise Resilient Kids*, we look at simple-to-follow, science-backed, and practical strategies and habits that will help parents raise mentally-strong, patient, and self-reliant kids. From helping them cope with uncertainties to failure and grief, we offer readers valuable insights to help kids overcome and recover from it. The book also features practical means to implement various strategies such as how to get them to become more confident, not fear making mistakes, take pride when owning up to them, and most important of all, learn to be resilient in tough times.

© **Copyright 2020 - All rights reserved.**

The content contained within this book may not be reproduced, duplicated or transmitted without direct written permission from the author or the publisher.

Under no circumstances will any blame or legal responsibility be held against the publisher, or author, for any damages, reparation, or monetary loss due to the information contained within this book, either directly or indirectly.

Legal Notice:

This book is copyright protected. It is only for personal use. You cannot amend, distribute, sell, use, quote or paraphrase any part, or the content within this book, without the consent of the author or publisher.

Disclaimer Notice:

Please note the information contained within this document is for educational and entertainment purposes only. All effort has been executed to present accurate, up to date, reliable, complete information. No warranties of any kind are declared or implied. Readers acknowledge that the author is not engaged in the rendering of legal, financial, medical or professional advice. The content within this book has been derived from various sources. Please consult a licensed professional before attempting any techniques outlined in this book.

By reading this document, the reader agrees that under no circumstances is the author responsible for any losses, direct or indirect, that are incurred as a result of the use of the information contained within this document, including, but not limited to, errors, omissions, or inaccuracies.

Before we begin, I have something special waiting for you. An action-packed 1 page printout with a few quick & easy tips taken from this book that you can start using today to become a better parent right now!

It's my gift to you, free of cost. Think of it as my way of saying thank you to you for purchasing this book.

Claim your download of Profoundly Positive Parenting with Frank Dixon by scanning the QR code below and join my mailing list.

Sign up below to grab your free copy, print it out and hang it on the fridge!

Sign Up By Scanning The QR Code With Your Phone's Camera To Be Redirected To A Page To Enter Your Email And Receive INSTANT Access To Your Download

ARE YOU BUSY?
LISTEN TO THE AUDIOBOOK
ANYTIME. ANYWHERE.

EXCLUSIVELY AVAILABLE ON audible

Give Audible a try!
Sign up by scanning the QR code with your phone's camera

With Audible you can listen to this book and others like it

Regular offers include:

- Try Audible for $0.00
- Access a growing selection of included Audible Originals, audiobooks and podcasts.

Fully flexible:

- Email reminder before your trial ends.
- 30 day trial.
- Cancel anytime.

Before we jump in, I'd like to express my gratitude. I know this mustn't be the first book you came across and yet you still decided to give it a read. There are numerous courses and guides you could have picked instead that promise to make you an ideal and well-rounded parent while raising your children to be the best they can be.

But for some reason, mine stood out from the rest and this makes me the happiest person on the planet right now. If you stick with it, I promise this will be a worthwhile read.

In the pages that follow, you're going to learn the best parenting skills so that your child can grow to become the best version of themselves and in doing so experience a meaningful understanding of what it means to be an effective parent.

Notable Quotes About Parenting

"Children Must Be Taught How To Think, Not What To Think."

— Margaret Mead

"It's easier to build strong children than to fix broken men [or women]."

- Frederick Douglass

"Truly great friends are hard to find, difficult to leave, and impossible to forget."

— George Randolf

"Nothing in life is to be feared, it is only to be understood. Now is the time to understand more, so that we may fear less."

— Scientist Marie Curie

Table of Contents

HOW PARENTS CAN RAISE RESILIENT CHILDREN 1

    Introduction 3

    Chapter 1: Understanding Resilience 6

    Chapter 2: All Kids Are Independent Thinkers .. 18

    Chapter 3: Taking Responsibility 32

    Chapter 4: Managing Big Feelings..................... 40

    Chapter 5: Time to Toughen Up! 48

    Conclusion...55

    References 58

HOW PARENTS CAN TEACH CHILDREN TO COUNTER NEGATIVE THOUGHTS 63

    Introduction 67

    Chapter 1: Into the Child's Mind 70

    Chapter 2: What Negativity Does to Your Child? 81

    Chapter 3: Am I Good Enough? 90

    Chapter 4: I Am Confident and Self-Reliant 96

Chapter 5: Taming
the Monster Under the Bed 102

Chapter 6: Call Upon the Stage—Willpower 109

Chapter 7: Resilience to the Rescue 114

Chapter 8: Is My Child Emotionally Ready? 119

Conclusion 124

References 126

HOW PARENTS CAN DEVELOP HAPPY CHILDREN 129

Introduction 133

Chapter 1: Social Skills – What Are They? 137

Chapter 2: Social Skills and Happiness –
Is There A Connection? 144

Chapter 3: Listening and Communication 153

Chapter 4: Empathy 165

Chapter 5: Manners
and Following Directions 174

Chapter 6: Making
Friends and Collaborative Play 183

Chapter 7: Responsibility and Cooperation 190

Conclusion 196

References 198

HOW PARENTS CAN TEACH CHILDREN TO LIVE WITH TRANSPARENCY 201

Introduction 205

Chapter 1: Being Honest – Is It Important? ... 208

Chapter 2: Lies, Lies, and More Lies… 215

Chapter 3: Preventing the Habit of Lying 221

Chapter 4: Ssshh, Don't Tell My Parents! 230

Chapter 5: What Am I Doing Wrong? 237

Chapter 6: Encouraging Openness 243

Chapter 7: Act like a Role Model - Period! 249

Chapter 8: Raising an Honest Child 255

Conclusion 261

References 263

HOW PARENTS CAN FOSTER FRIENDSHIP IN CHILDREN 267

Introduction 271

Chapter 1: Understanding Friendship 273

Chapter 2: Essential Friendship Building Skills 281

Chapter 3: How to Make Friends 288

Chapter 4: Friendships in School 296

Chapter 5: Friendships at Home 302

Chapter 6: Fostering Healthy Bonds 312

Chapter 7: Friendship FAQs 319

Conclusion.. 324
References 326

HOW PARENTS CAN RAISE RESILIENT CHILDREN

Preparing Your Child for the Real Tough World of Adulthood by Instilling Them With Principles of Love, Self-Discipline, and Independent Thinking

FRANK DIXON

Introduction

Sometimes, parenting is a lot like being in the war. You are the one leading the army into the unknown with a plan you have well-thought-of but still doubt. But what you forget to take into account is the enemy also has a plan that defies yours, and now you have to rethink your plan and strategies and devise a new one. But wait, the enemy gets the hint of it too and they are onto something mischievous themselves...

Ahh, this never ends. There are no martyrs and, at the end of the day, the enemy often sleeps better with their tummies full.

Parenting isn't easy and that is the nicest way to put it. It is walking in heels in the sand with a tray full of expensive champagne in it. It is finding that one sock in the whole house when you already have it on. You want silence and some peace, but you also know it means something suspicious is going on. You feel like you haven't bathed in years or worn heels or put on makeup and all these things, which, once were the norm now seem a luxury. There are no time-outs. It's a full-time job you joyously applied for and are now rethinking your mental state at that time. Plus, there are no paid leaves, vacations, bonuses, or even recognition for all the hard work you put in because that is just how cruel the world is.

It keeps pulling your leg over things you barely have control over and insists on declaring you a failure.

And sometimes, it isn't someone from the outside; it is that inner voice that demotivates you and reminds you that you should do better the next time. But aren't we all trying our best already? It didn't seem that hard in the past, did it? Were we as crazy, hyperactive, and disobedient? Or was there something else that made us turn up this beautiful specimen? We weren't always nagging for things or crying over spilled milk (literally) and our parents never seemed to have any trouble raising us. Just a look of theirs and it would send shivers down our spine and we prayed to God to not be spanked the minute we got home.

Parenting has evolved over the years. We no longer have the same family structures and hierarchy. Our parents had help from their parents and relatives to raise us. We all lived nearby, and remember how they used to say, "It takes a whole village to raise a kid?" Well, it was very much like that. Kids were taught different values than the ones they are taught today. They were told to behave, stay disciplined, and be strong and tough. Today, they are taught to be more open, be active and inquisitive, and be whom they want to be. Don't get us wrong, there is no harm in any of these values but the way they are instilled upon kids is debatable.

Some parents give their kids complete liberty of writing their destiny, thinking they are smart to figure things out on their own. It may work for some, but most kids require direction and some disciplining. Discipline, bring synonymous to teaching and not punishment. They need a mentor, a role model, and a teacher to help them distinguish between right and wrong, help them build a strong character and face overwhelming emotions and challenges with self-control and logic. These are the virtues we, as parents, should bestow upon our kids. It is upon us to show them the path and then leave it up to them to decide when they want to start their journey and where they need to stop. We have to teach them to be independent, in control, resilient, and emotionally intellectual. Only then will they be ready for the tough world.

Together, in this book, we shall look at different ways to make kids ready for the competitive, ever-evolving, and challenging world that will pull them down if they are not resilient enough. Each chapter talks of a different value, the crucial role it plays in their development, and how kids can take them up with some help from their parents.

So, without further ado, let's get right into it, shall we?

Chapter 1: Understanding Resilience

We have been using the word resilience for a long time now. It has different meanings in different applications. For instance, in biology, resilience is used to define the ability of an organism in an environment filled with predators and uncertainty. In ecology, researchers used the term to define an ecosystem's capacity to sustain its functions without being disturbed and, in case of any disturbance, returning to its natural/original state. In metallurgy, we use it to define a metal's property to resist when prone to shocks.

A French scientist, Boris Cyrulnik, first used the word to describe a human's ability to move on or carry on regardless of what trauma, breakdown, or failure it faced. So, in simpler terms, we can assume that resilience refers to having the ability to bounce back or not become affected by something after it has happened. It is about moving on and reconstructing ourselves post-shock or tragedy. Fortunately, it isn't a personality trait but rather a skill that can be nurtured and polished. Everyone has resilience. It is only a question of how much and whether we put it to good use or not when faced with trauma, failure, or tragedy. It doesn't mean that one doesn't find situations too intense, overwhelming, heartbreaking, or difficult to deal with. It is just how they respond to it and cope with it. People who are more resilient get over it quicker than those who aren't resilient enough.

As it is a skill, building or encouraging its use is achievable. It may take some time, effort, and patience, but it will happen. However, thinking that some significant change will happen overnight or after reading some inspirational book about it will make you resilient is fallacious. Whoever suggests this lacks knowledge or experience.

Embracing Resilience

The reason resilience in kids is becoming such a hot topic these days is because the world is becoming tougher by the day. There is more competition than ever and poor self-esteem and coping skills are not going to help them face it. They need to have the right direction, essential resources, and mental strength to find their place in it despite the challenges and hardships. They need to embrace and practice becoming resilient because things will only get harsher. But why resilience?

If we were to see what resilience in kids looks like, here are some characteristics they will hopefully possess. We shall let you decide if these are qualities you would want your kids to have or not.

Resilient children are socially adept. They know how to reach out to others for help such as caregivers, adults, or peers and establish stronger bonds with them. They find comfort in being social and are more open and communicative.

Resilient children possess more control of their emotions, feelings, and their reactions to those emotions and feelings. They have the leverage to influence situations and confront problems independently and confidently. They don't give up easily and continue to try and work on their inadequacies.

Resilient children are also optimistic. They don't face challenges with a cynical attitude. They are the ones who find something positive even amidst failures. For example, if forced to move cities and make new friends, a resilient kid won't feel shy or hold grudges against their parents. Instead, they will welcome the change positively and accept the new place and people open-heartedly. They feel fully prepared for whatever life throws at them and are excited rather than scared or worried when something challenging comes up.

Resilient children also believe their lives are purposeful. They don't see struggles or challenges as the reason to end it or give up hope. They set big goals in life, aren't afraid to follow their passions, and accept failure when it happens. For example, a kid who wants to stand first in class will work harder and give their best when it comes to assignments and projects even if they have a difficult time with them at the start.

Finally, resilient children also have great problem-solving skills. They don't hide their talents or skills and look for solutions to problems creatively and persistently. At the same time, they are also flexible in their attempts and don't always go by the book and take the required action. An example of this would be Casey, a three-year-old trying to open her toy basket. She doesn't give up after two attempts like her brother but continues to try to open the basket with every technique she can come up with. Ultimately, she kicks it hard enough so it falls on the ground and opens up itself. Yes, we know it isn't the best of examples as you will have to clean up the mess of all the toys on the carpet, but you have to appreciate the effort and technique.

The Need for Raising Resilient Kids

That being said, one simply can't overlook the benefits being resilient offers and the sooner you start with the principles, the better. When children are young, so are their minds. It isn't developed fully and thus able to absorb more and adapt. Did you know that by the time your kid starts kindergarten, 95% of their mind is fully developed? This means the sooner we begin with resilience-building habits, the better.

Besides, resilience doesn't stop them from trying new things or playing safe to avoid failure, heartbreak, or tragedy. It isn't meant to eliminate stress but rather, accept setbacks and pain as it comes. Just because someone is resilient doesn't mean they see the world with colored lenses. They just adapt to the aftermath better than others and learn to cope on their own. Like others, they experience grief and sadness that comes when they fight with their best friend, they too experience pain when they have to get flu shots at the doctor's, they too fear uncertainty when picking chits for who their science partner be… it is only that their mental outlook makes them competent to work through those difficult times and recover.

Therapist Joshua Miles has suggested some benefits of raising resilient kids which are worth giving a read. Take a look to convince yourself and your partner why you should start teaching them about resilience, even if they are just five years old. According to Miles, resilient kids:

- Show improved learning and greater academic achievement
- Take less offs from school due to sickness as they can recover sooner
- Demonstrate reduced risk-taking behaviors
- Are less likely to indulge in excessive drinking, using drugs, or smoking
- Have a lower mortality rate and better overall well-being and health
- Are family or community-oriented and empathic towards others

The Seven Cs of Building Resilience in Kids

Kenneth Ginsburg, a renowned pediatrician at the Philadelphia Children's Hospital believes every child tries to live up to the expectations we set for them. They are always looking up to adults who believe in their capabilities unconditionally and guide them with compassion and generosity. In his book, *Building Resilience and Children and Teens*, he talks about how all kids, young or old, require encouragement from their peers and parents to believe in the ideas they have and put them into practice. He further argues that if kids are only thinking about fitting in a box, they will never be able to think outside it, and thus, not do something extraordinary with their lives. They need to be encouraged and motivated to think in new ways and build resilience over time. He suggests using the seven Cs of resilience to raise them as mentally-tough and creative beings.

Competence

Children often seek recognition when they do something well. They want that clap and pat on the back from their parents and peers. Additionally, they also look for opportunities to cultivate new skills and foster talents. As parents, it is our job to provide them with ample opportunities to succeed and flourish. Here are some ideas on how you, as an adult, can help them develop competence:

- Focus on the strengths they possess and not highlight their weaknesses

- Tell them when they have made a mistake but in a positive manner. (I see you have accomplished the task well, but do you know if you had done it this way, it would have taken less time?)

- Empower them to make their decisions themselves. Let them come up with solutions to a problem individualistically.

- Don't suffocate them with your worry and concern. Of course, you want to protect them and keep them safe, but often when parents are too involved in a child's life, they start to feel incompetent. If there are things they can do themselves, let them handle them on their own.

- Avoid comparing them with other siblings or kids their age.

Confidence

Your goal as a parent is to boost your child's talents and skills so they feel confident when attempting them. If they think you believe they can hit the ball out of the court, they might do it. Why? Because they feel confident! That confidence is a product of your faith and belief in their skills and abilities that makes them push for things that are sometimes unachievable. Here are some ways you can build confidence in them:

- Focus on the best things about your child's personality so they start to see that as well
- Teach them about fairness, persistence, integrity, and kindness
- Avoid pushing them to do something they are not comfortable attempting or feel like they can't handle it
- Praise honestly like you mean it when they achieve something – even if it is the hundredth time they do it

Connection

Children want to feel like they belong somewhere. They want to feel like they aren't alone and want to cultivate meaningful connections with everyone if given the chance. Therefore, as parents, it is your job to not push them away when they come to us with their problems or struggles with something. To help them build connections with everyone around them without hesitance or fear of being disregarded, here's what you need to do:

- Ensure they are safe and always looked after physically
- Allow them the liberty to be as expressive as they want to be when it comes to big

emotions. For instance, don't ask them to quiet down when they are upset about something or feel like crying. Instead, offer them ideas on how they can cope with what they are feeling in more productive ways

- Resolve problems as they arise by addressing conflict openly
- Make your house welcoming to all forms of communication. Designate an area where the family can share time and have a decent conversation
- Foster healthy relationships that promote positive messages

Character

Every kid needs a moral compass to follow and a basic understanding of what's right and what's not. This shows them they can't be put down for who they are. To build a strong character in them, begin with:

- Showing them they are empathetic and caring
- Demonstrating how negative behaviors can sometimes cloud judgment and make things difficult
- Preaching the importance of community and the perks of helping others

- Eliminating stereotyping or racial discriminations and raising them as morally-sound

Contribution

Kids are naturally empathetic. They will come to comfort you when they see you upset. It is their natural tendency to contribute in some way. Therefore, when they come to you and present you with a get well soon card or a hug, don't disregard them. They want to be of service and even if you think you need to be alone, let them know politely. When they feel valued, they will continue to be of help. They also learn how good it feels to be able to help and don't feel shy asking for it either. This is one important aspect of becoming resilient – that you seek help without any shame or guilt. Here's how you can encourage them to contribute more:

- Communicate with them how many people in the world lack necessities like food and shelter so they learn to be compassionate and not act privileged

- Stress how important it is to be of service to others

- Model generosity yourself and always choose to discipline with empathy (more on this is the next chapter)

- Create opportunities that allow them to contribute or ask for their help with the chores so they learn to contribute innately

Coping

Children also need to learn some coping mechanisms against stress, so they know when to engage or disengage themselves from things and people. When they learn better coping mechanisms, they will be more prepared to face adversity and ultimately get over it. Below are a few ways to teach them how to cope better:

- Model positive coping strategies as kids learn what they see
- Teach them how to implement coping strategies consistently such as what to do when they feel angry, sad, or emotionally-troubled
- Understand that whatever negative behavior your child is depicting is due to some underlying stress about something and, therefore, be empathetic.
- Understand that telling them to stop that negative behavior is only going to make matters worse, and therefore, try to distract them in some other way so they become engaged elsewhere.

Control

Children who are aware they are the ones in control of their decisions are likelier to bounce back after something tragic. When they feel in control, they know that whatever they choose to do is their own doing, and thus, no one else should be blamed but them. This type of behavior is also prominent in adults. When we think our mistakes are our own, we face them willingly. We know it was no one's doing but our own that failed, and thus, we are quick to pick up ourselves. As parents, we can encourage the same in the following manner:

- Help them comprehend that everything happening to them isn't purely random whilst also teaching them that not everything is under our control, and therefore, we shouldn't hold ourselves accountable all the time.

- Also, use discipline and compassion to teach them anything new. They don't need to see you controlling or punishing you because they will adopt the same behavior.

Chapter 2: All Kids Are Independent Thinkers

According to Linda S. Gottfredson, an education professor at the University of Delaware, intelligence reflects how we process information, learn, understand, and reason things (Gottfredson, 1996). There is no means to tell that a kid with its head submerged in books will be smarter than the one roaming the streets. There is no means to measure how they process new information, what they learn from it, and how they make use of that newfound knowledge.

This is why some kids are street-smart while others enjoy the reading bit. It is why some of them are interested in painting pictures and others in building towers with blocks. It is why some kids are the school's favorite footballers while some are everyone's friend and know how to make others feel better.

Every child is unique and creative in their ways, and as adults, it is our job to hone that creativity and uniqueness in them so they can find a place for themselves in this world. It is our job to encourage and motivate them to follow their passions and not force them into doing or taking up things they aren't interested in. There is little chance your son will do well with cello lessons if all he wants is to play soccer. It is less likely that someone who doesn't like ballet will be good at it. Therefore, as parents, the first thing you need to do is stop comparing your kids to someone else. They are unique in their way and thus don't need to be bullied or forced to go to that next practice session if they want to take up the stage and become a performer. Just because someone else's kid is doing it doesn't mean yours have to, too.

Even though we know that comparison doesn't sit well with everyone, it is especially debasing for little ones. Kids are tender and less emotionally-intelligent when young. They don't adhere well to criticism, especially when it comes to people they trust the most. There is always some better way of telling them to improve or do better than rubbing their face in their shortcomings or mistakes.

Many parents argue that it is quite natural to want to know where their kids stand amongst others and what percentages they have or what ranks they hold so when the time comes to bid for a coveted seat in a top university, they know they aren't making a fool of themselves. True, but does that mean you get the right to parade them in front of others like decorative pieces and ask them to show off their skill and harangue them when they don't do well? This is the very practice that makes them develop an inferiority complex. Other than that:

Comparison leads to the kid withdrawing themselves from others and social gatherings (Rubin, Coplan, & Bowker, 2009). They create this idea in their head that no matter how hard they try, someone will upstage them and outperform, so there is no point in trying and becoming a laughing stock.

It also causes self-doubt where the kids start to question if they will ever be anything but average or not. They feel there is nothing they can excel at and thus give up before even trying.

Secondly, it lowers their self-esteem and eats away their confidence. They start to question their self-worth when they don't think of themselves as good enough. They feel like they lack the abilities and skills other kids their age have. These lead to unwanted stress and depression in their lives and ultimately lead to multiple mental health issues at a young age (Solomons, 2013).

Thirdly, it lays roots of jealousy and rivalry. When being compared to an apparent paragon of virtue incessantly, they develop hatred and jealousy towards them. Jealousy is never a positive expression and thus must never be cultivated. It can lead to aggressiveness in kids.

And finally, it suppresses their talents and skills. When they are not appreciated for who they are and what makes them unique, their talents don't blossom either and they eventually lose them.

So, treat them with kindness and compassion so they can confidently put their skills and talents to good use.

Putting the C in Creativity

Many researchers today believe it is our doing that kids are no longer creative. Wondering why they think such a thing? Well, ask yourself this: when you were little, did you have as many toys as kids of today have? Did they spend all their time confined in homes or glued to screens for hours without notice? Even though the goal of toy companies is to improve the overall experience of play for kids, they are unintentionally reaping them off their imagination. Children no longer indulge in pretend-play and make-believe games. They have everything in the palm of their hands already. The same can be said for adolescents and teenagers. Just a swipe on their phones and they are introduced to all the knowledge and entertainment in the world there is.

Kids have powerful imaginations but, like a car engine, they need proper fueling. This feeling comes in the form of encouragement and believes in their abilities. Since the goal is to help them develop resilience, we had to look and find if there was a connection between creativity and resilience or not. Interestingly, there is.

According to one study, kids who are more creative thinkers cope with pain and stress better (Reznick, 2009). They are more confident in their approaches to deal with any hardship and challenge, have better social skills that enable them to seek guidance and help, and are better learners and problem-solvers.

So, how do you cultivate creativity if that is what makes them resilient? Here are a few ideas worth trying.

Offer them the resources they need to express their creative side. Give them an ample amount of unstructured time for imaginative play. Secondly, give them space both physical and mental to attempt things independently. Don't mind creative clutter. Let them pull out every toy from the basket, stay in their rooms or up in the attic playing and imagining things.

Let curiosity be their guide and take them to new places. Encourage their intrigue to know more about any and everything. Take them to places that will broaden their knowledge like museums. Don't shush them up when they bother you with a million "whys."

Most importantly, never underestimate, mock, or dismiss their ideas. No idea is ever a stupid one. Mocking or ridiculing an idea discredits their creativity and they may feel incompetent. Their idea may be bogus but it can still hold some merit in terms of the concept, thought process, or rationale. Work with them to polish and nurture it with them.

Avoid acting bossy or trying to modify their ideas by adding your touch to them. Kids don't need that. Give them the freedom and autonomy to explore them on their own. If they want to go to every neighbor's house to feed their dog because they want to, don't tell them it isn't safe and clutch them to your chest fearing their safety. Instead, ask them if they would like you to accompany them and hold the treats for them. If the kid is older and wishes to spend a night at a friend, ask them if they would let you drive them there and have a small talk with their parents.

Moreover, let them make mistakes and don't intervene too much. Some studies show that when parents are too eager to get involved in their child's life, they reduce flexibility in thinking. It is alright if they aren't able to put the puzzle together on their own. Don't do it for them unless asked to. They will eventually get it one day. Another way of putting this is problem-solving with them and not for them. We hope you understand the difference between the two.

Lastly, encourage messing around. Not all imagination takes place in the head; some of it takes place on the ground too. New ideas are bound to emerge when they are given the right tools to play with. After all, there can be more ways of building a tower than just stacking one block on top of the other.

But They Have to be Disciplined, Right?

As parents, disciplining our kids is one of the most important responsibilities we have. We may like to be their friend, but we also have to be a disciplinarian at times. Shockingly, when parents come for counseling and are advised to discipline their kids, a majority of them mistake it for spanking, yelling, and strict punishments. But the term discipline never meant that originally. It is us who have modified it to mean "punishment." Originally, the word discipline was derived from a Latin word, which translated to "to teach." Disciplining children is a teaching process. How we choose to do it depends on our parenting style. We are going to discuss three of the most common ones and you will see that only one of them is what teaches kids to become resilient.

Are you authoritarian?

Authoritarian parents often seek yelling and spanking as the primary means to discipline their kids. There is no room for negotiation or explanation. If the child has done something wrong, they will be punished for it – no ifs and buts.

Are you permissive?

As the name suggests, permissive parents allow permission to make mistakes without setting consequences for it. They let their children be their boss and rule the roost. However, this often leads to the child thinking their parents don't care about them enough and are always disinterested. Some adults who have been brought up in such households wished to have some set limits. In simpler words, permissive parents don't believe in disciplining their kids.

Are you authoritative?

Finally, we have authoritative parenting, which is slightly different than both parenting styles mentioned above. Authoritative parents are those who set firm limits, have some room for healthy discussion, and realize it is their job to teach self-discipline. So, they allow their children to do whatever they want to do but also tell them the consequences of their actions. For example, telling your child to go to bed early so they don't miss the school bus and walk to school is authoritative parenting. You are giving them the choice to pick a certain behavior but also telling them where it would lead them. It involves teaching them to be their boss but also facing the consequences of their actions and owning up to them when the time comes. This is what makes them self-disciplined and resilient, don't you think?

But why do we discipline kids in the first place? Is it because we want them to give up certain behaviors? Is it because we want them to excel at everything in their future? Is it because we want to teach them the difference between right and wrong or good or bad?

Most parents discipline their kids because they want them to grow up as responsible, wise, and honest adults. But before we learn of the many techniques to discipline that doesn't involve punishments, we need to understand why kids misbehave.

Children often misbehave, disobey, or disregard their parents' advice because they feel emotionally-stimulated. They feel too much and too often and don't know what to make of those feelings. They feel jealous when another sibling gets more attention, they feel frustrated and angry when being compared with others, and they feel upset because they feel unheard and uncared for. As they are young, their limbic system is developed more than their frontal cortex, which regulates emotions. This means the emotions they feel are stronger than what their minds can handle or cope with. Their frontal cortex only starts developing when they pass toddlerhood.

Setting Limits and Consequences Without Punishments

Now that we understand some of what goes on inside their tiny heads, we continue from where we left off – techniques that discipline kids without punishing them. The reason we insist on positive disciplining is that when kids are faced with big emotions and don't know what to do about them, they do what they know: cry, throw a tantrum, or become aggressive. We perceive these actions as an act of misbehavior and become too rigid and harsh. Kids can start to fear such a response, which is something no parent wants. So, when it comes to disciplining them, here are some ideas to take note of.

Be Their Role Model

They need to learn to regulate their emotions and act resiliently in difficult times. And who can teach them better than their parents? But the question is: what do you do when faced with hardships? Because believe it or not, chances are your kids are going to pick up the same response. Therefore, if you have the habit of yelling, screaming, cursing, and isolating yourself in times of hardship, your kids are going to do that too. So, the first rule is to learn to self-regulate your emotions. They need to understand that emotions are natural and shouldn't be hidden or run away from. They allow us to set boundaries by determining what we are okay with and with what we aren't.

Nourish the Parent-Child Relationship

No matter how young or old your kids are, they will always come to you with their problems. They may not be too forward when they are older, but their changed behavior is a sign that something isn't right. Therefore, for parents, it is imperative that a strong parent-child relationship is built from an early age so the child views their parents as their mentor and guide. Kids will always try their hardest to impress you. They will rarely deliberately try to disappoint you. Multiple research studies suggest that when a strong parent-child relationship is prevalent, kids are less likely to misbehave. It isn't fear of their anger that makes them well-behaved but rather the sanctity of the special bond. They don't want to do anything that would upset the stability of the bond. This connection has to be fostered with care in terms of soothing, connecting with them frequently, and correcting them with empathy.

Be Their Behavior Mentor

Just a made-up word, but what it stands for is important. If you wish to instill discipline, you have to be more loving and caring. Kids are more receptive when spoken to with love and treated with care and interest. Their brains blank out the minute they are scolded by their parents or teachers. This eliminates the need for it as it doesn't guarantee any favorable results. It is a universal fact that when we are stressed out, our brain stops to process new information clearly and we are less likely to make sane decisions.

Love Can Go a Long Way

If you take a look at all those studies done on resilient people, you will be surprised to know that many of them rated companionship of someone who trusted in them and stood by them without judgment the highest. As kids look up their parents and peers, they seek acceptance and recognition. They want to be cared for, loved, and heard. It is very difficult to love one's self if no one else does. So, surrounding yourself with people who love you, accept you, and correct you without being accusatory and judgmental is essential. You always turn to them in times of adversity and are assured they will come to your rescue. When we feel safe or understand what it feels like, we develop an optimistic outlook. We become more caring and devoted to others. We want to support others too and be there for them in times of need. We take into account what they are going through and offer aid and compassion.

This is what empathy is all about. Teaching something new with empathy and love is more likely to stick with them. Picture this: your child is going through a rough patch. They have just broken up with their best friend and are worried if they will ever talk to them again. Instead of being negative or judgmental, if you decide to be empathetic, sit them down, and try to be in their shoes when offering solutions, it will be received well. On the other hand, if you treat them with condescending views or disregard their problem as something petty, there is little chance they will come to you the next time.

Thus, reaching out to them with empathy is what seems like an ideal solution whether you are trying to treat misbehavior, negative emotions, or instill new habits. How can being empathetic make you a better teacher to stem new habits like resilience, self-discipline, and independence? Let's see!

Implanting New Habits With Love and Empathy

Be a Coach, But Don't Coach

Sounds confusing, but hear us out. You want them to obey you, follow your commands, and take up good habits but not while you order them to. Coaches help children develop and enhance skills, but it is they who have to play the game and show how well they have been taught. As a parent, you have to act as their mentor and teach them rather than doing things for them. The only way to build resilience is if they have confidence in themselves to get over things. Don't rob them of the opportunity to learn competence.

Aim for Progress and Not Perfection

If it is something new you are teaching them, don't expect them to become masters of it overnight. Teaching new habits like resilience, emotional-intelligence, and independence take time and effort. So, don't push too hard, and aim for progress and improvement. Too much pressure can undermine their confidence.

Teach Independence by Allowing Them to be Independent

Many teachers believe the best way to teach someone something new is to let them experience it hands-on. You can't learn to swim if you are afraid of the water. Don't abandon them completely but encourage trying new things. Stay back and watch from a distance how well or poorly they do it. Offer aid only when asked and don't forget to appreciate it.

Empathize and Praise Descriptively

Instead of just saying, "Good job," give them something more and meaningful to be happy about. Tell them what they did well and why you think it was brilliant. Descriptive praise helps hone all those areas they are experts in. Also, don't forget to empathize and appreciate accordingly. Tell them how proud you are they pulled XYZ off and how hard it must have been for them. Tell them how happy you are they didn't give up and strived to become better.

Chapter 3: Taking Responsibility

Do you recall the first time you held them in your arms? You swore to yourself that you will let no harm come to them. Ever since then, you have loved them unconditionally, watched them grow, cried with them when they were hurt, played nonsensical games with them for hours, worried about their health, nutrition, and well-being, helped them crawl, stand, and walk on their two feet, and offered them comfort and your warm embrace whenever they came crying to you over something. As parents, we all want to nurture our kids, keep them safe from harm, and teach them the best values so when they grow up, they are ready for the world.

But amidst doing so, we have, and we are talking about every parent here, sometimes shielded them from making mistakes. We have been to the rescue before they did something wrong or harmful. Although you aren't to blame here, did you know that whenever you did that, you deprived them of a great learning opportunity to grow and build resilience (Oosthuizen, 2020)? To raise them as healthy, capable, emotionally-intellectual, and confident individuals, we have to let them make mistakes. But, of course, own up to them too!

When do children make mistakes? When they do something the way it shouldn't have been done. Usually, errors result in failure, which leads to stress and the buildup of negative emotions. But despite that, children must be given every opportunity to struggle so even if they fail, they develop emotional and coping skills. Many psychologists associate coping skills as muscles. We can never know how strong we are unless we use them.

Historically, many educators believed that to perfect one's development of skills, the best way was to eliminate the creation of mistakes. It made sense for some time and many other educators followed suit too but things started to change when researchers and child specialists observed how crucial a role mistakes play in fostering resilience. Even today, we don't deliberately set up our kids for failure. We have this premeditated notion to make things easier for them so they can do without making mistakes. Unconsciously, we all discourage mistakes as we feel it is synonymous with failure. So, we drill the right answers into them by repeating the question over and over again until they memorize it and pray that they do well in a standardized test too. Because God forbid, who can afford poor grades even though the child has zero knowledge about the concepts and foundation of things?

Recent studies suggest that learning improves when kids make mistakes as their curiosity to know what is right is heightened. Every form of learning is enriched via error. Ask yourself this: if they won't choose the wrong friends first, how will they know how to choose the right ones? If they won't wear the left shoe in their right foot and fall, how will they know to put the right shoe in the right foot the next time? Making mistakes challenges kids to do better. Rarely do mistakes result in them giving up. Mistakes motivate them to think differently, come up with a new possible solution or explanation for things. It makes their mind go in turbo-charge mode to attempt things differently. Isn't that what learning should look like? It should be fun, challenging, and a driving force to discover new possibilities and approaches.

According to Carol Dweck, the author of the bestseller, *Mindset: The New Psychology of Success* and a professor at Stanford University, children must always be challenged one way or another to enhance learning. Even when they repeatedly make mistakes, parents' shouldn't try to make things easier for them and rather let them come up with new strategies and means to handle them. Did you know, her research suggests that when parents repetitively praise children for their intelligence rather than their problem-solving skills, they are less likely to remain persistent in the face of a challenge? This conclusion was derived after her team of experts followed up with 100+ 5th graders in the best schools of NYC. In her book, she writes about the experiment in detail to encourage parents to praise kids over their efforts – even if they fail – and not their intelligence, which happens to be a genetic trait. To briefly sum up her experiment, she divided the participating 5th graders into two groups. One group was appreciated for their intelligence while the other for their effort.

As it turns out, when faced with a challenging test designed for 8th graders, children who were praised for their efforts performed harder despite making numerous mistakes. They seemed more determined to take on the task and tried their best to perform better. On the other hand, children who were praised for their intelligence were soon to feel like a failure as the more mistakes they made, the more discouraged they got.

This proved that parents who praised results more than efforts don't raise resilient kids. Instead, what they raise are kids who are too scared to disappoint that they don't even give their best shot at things. Therefore, if you are doing the same, you can't expect them to grow up to become resilient as they lack the skills to accept failure and come out of it. Moreover, Dweck also believes parents shouldn't be too quick to praise or put down their children as they lose important opportunities for learning.

Did I Do Something Wrong?

A mistake can be anatomized as a decision or action we soon come to regret. Mistakes come paired with some form of loss, pain, and struggle. No one, not even adults are in favor of what consequences it brings along. But that doesn't mean we never make one. We all do! Sometimes, graver than the ones made by our kids. But the irony is that mistakes are one of the things we try hard not to stumble upon and yet sometimes, also the most important things we need to experience.

As we don't like to be reminded of our mistakes from time to time, so do our kids. Parents who have the habit of bringing up their children's mistakes in front of others to joke or ridicule them are setting them up for poor self-worth and low self-esteem. Kids who are often mocked by one or both their parents exhibit unstable mental health as they feel they are not good enough. As parents, we shouldn't bring up past mistakes to degrade our kids as no one likes to deliberately make them. Besides, as we have already established that making mistakes can be good; we have to format our responses accordingly.

Watching our kids make a blunder is never easy. Knowing that what they are doing is wrong, it is hard to resist the temptation of making things better for them. Of course, your instinct is to save them from trauma, pain, or hurt later, but perhaps it is best to let them navigate their way themselves. When they spring back from mistakes with techniques they came up with, it boosts their sense of confidence in their abilities.

So, instead of focusing solely on what they did wrong, we should try to focus on helping them cope with the emotions that follow after. How will they cope with anger, frustration, or guilt after they have made a mistake? Well, that is where you step in. But before we do that, make sure you do the following:

Say Thank You

If they come up to you to admit they have made a boo-boo, thank them for it. Of course, it will boil your blood when they tell you what they have done but this is the moment when you have to overlook their mistake and praise them for their honesty. This gives children an open window for communication as they feel they can come up to you with whatever troubles them and be expressive about it. This also teaches them you will offer help rather than a sound scolding, which instills the idea that they always have someone they can count on.

Encourage Risk-Taking

Your kid should be trying something new every day to broaden their knowledge and learning. They shouldn't worry about making mistakes or becoming scared of failure. Show them it is okay to step out of their comfort zones and give new things a try.

Be Vocal About Their Efforts

If you have only been praising them over an A+ grade or win in the spelling bee contest, you are amplifying their fears of trying new things. They start to believe that if they try something new, they will surely fail. This makes them dependent and less resilient. So, applaud their efforts even if they fail to achieve the desired results. This will make them persistent and more willing to take on new challenges without the fear of failure.

Tell Them a Secret

To instill the habit of owning up to their mistakes, share with them mistakes you made when you were their age and how you coped with them. Tell them in detail how you handled them, owned up them, and made required compensations to prevent repeating them. When kids make mistakes, they feel like failures. They think they are incapable of handling things. But having someone tell them they aren't the only ones to make mistakes drills a sense of comfort in them and gives them a boost to do better.

Teach Them Accountability

One of the greatest things one can do when they have faulted is to accept responsibility for their actions and be accountable. In case our mistakes have hurt someone, it is our job to apologize and pay our condolences. Your kids should be taught the same from an early age so they learn an important life lesson – fixing something that has been broken at the right time. They must acknowledge that their actions resulted in someone getting hurt and therefore, it is now their job to make amends. This also allows them to move past the grief, shame, and guilt they feel. It also shows them that everything can be made better if one tries hard enough.

Teach Them to Trace Back

Kids need to know what mistakes they made and where. If you want them to claim responsibility for their blunders, ask them what they did and what happened afterward. The second part of the sentence is to remind them to trace back and know what action resulted in the mistake, so the next time, they avoid repeating it.

Tell Them What's Done Is Done

There is no point holding onto the faults. Kids shouldn't think that just because they have made a mistake, it is the end of the world. Instead, tell them it is just the beginning of learning. For example, if they lost a race on sports day, instead of putting them down, encourage them to try harder the next time, get a coach, or try a different technique. But be mindful as you don't want to hand them the solutions on a plate; you need to encourage them to brainstorm ideas themselves.

Be Their Accountability Partner

If you want them to avoid repeating the same mistakes over and over again, someone has to keep them in check and navigate their way with them. Be their accountability partner so you remain aware that they haven't fully given up something because they made a blunder the last time and also to remind them to work harder as you are counting on them. Create chore lists and place them in visible places where they can see them. Be sure to mention the mistake they made the last time in a subtle but clear manner. For example, if the last time they forgot to separate their laundry in white and blacks, a little reminder suggesting to sort properly can go a long way.

Chapter 4: Managing Big Feelings

Mentally-strong and resilient kids are in control of their feelings and emotions. They know how to remain sane and take critical decisions at the right time without letting their emotions and internal feelings cloud their judgment. They know how to regulate them accordingly. They don't let their emotions overpower them or become the controller. As this looks like a favorable skill, it is ideal to develop it in your kids too. They too should know how to handle their reactions and form better responses. They too should know how to keep negative emotions at bay.

But here is where the problem lies. Kids aren't born with an understanding of emotions. Their lack of vocabulary further escalates the problem as they aren't able to put into words what they are going through. So, to expect them to be socially-appropriate when expressing themselves is a little too much to ask. This is one reason why child specialists and counselors suggest starting as early as possible to build resilience. So, when they are faced with a challenging situation or emotion, they know how to handle it appropriately.

When children aren't taught to self-regulate their emotions and manage their responses and behaviors, they often resort to aggressive behaviors to have their demands fulfilled. However, when they are denied that liberty, they bring out the angry face and start to throw things or create a scene. This portrays bad parenting. Besides, no child should be left to feel sad all by themselves for hours at a time over some small loss like the death of their best caterpillar. No matter how big the challenge or hardship, they should know how to handle it.

Another reason why learning to regulate emotions is essential is because when kids don't understand what they are experiencing, they avoid feeling that way. They start to avoid situations that will yield similar emotions. This fear of attempting anything outside of their comfort zones can limit their potential to soar high and be prepared to fly away from the nest, aka be prepared for the tough world outside. For instance, someone who doesn't do well in big social circles will try their best to avoid interactions as they don't feel comfortable. When the same kid starts school or heads for college, they will never be the first ones to raise their hand despite knowing the answer to a question or join an activity with lots of classmates. Their lack of confidence and fear of being social will limit their chances of success.

Feelings can be overwhelming, even for adults. Imagine how hard it must be for our little ones. They are still only learning so much every minute of the day, and being introduced to some foreign emotion, it can become challenging, to say the least.

Developing Coping Skills

Without the self-regulation of emotions, kids are going to act out. They are just being kids by saying, "Since we feel out of control, we shall act like it too." Therefore, strong coping skills should be harnessed to make them independent and self-reliant. Kids who aren't taught how to manage emotions the right way learn it themselves and they aren't always guaranteed to be the best. For instance, some adults fall into the habit of drinking and drug addiction because they are unable to cope with how they feel. They resort to self-harming practices that further take them down the dark pit. No parent in their right mind would want to see their kid grow up to be like that. Therefore, to avoid the chances of them picking up unhealthy coping strategies, be the torchbearer they need in their lives to navigate the way.

It is also observed that children with unhealthy coping mechanisms also exhibit avoidance coping. Avoidance coping can be defined as avoiding one activity and indulging in another to make oneself feel better. If we were to see an example of it, it would look something like this: a child ditching their homework to go outside and play ball with their friends because they don't possess the requisite problem-solving skills to do it. So, they avoid the activity altogether because playing ball makes them feel more relaxed and in control. Just because they didn't try to learn to handle their anxiety around math homework, they are willing to further fall behind in school.

According to one study, kids who use avoidance coping are at a higher risk of using marijuana as they grow up (Hyman & Sinha, 2008). Those who lack the basic problem-solving skills and are ready to put their hands up in the air and surrender showed lifetime marijuana use. This shows that the lack of proper coping strategies can lead to dependence on life-threatening things like substance abuse.

On a positive note, children who develop strong coping skills are more resilient in general and enjoy better opportunities in life. They have better overall well-being and are more social and empathetic in nature as opposed to those who haven't developed the right coping strategies (Jones, Greenberg, & Crowley, 2015). The same study also suggested that kids who had learned to regulate their emotions at the supple age of five were more likely to enroll in college and have steady high-paying jobs. They are also less likely to indulge in criminal activities, report mental health problems, and/or become engaged in substance abuse.

Strategies to Manage Riotous Emotions at an Early Age

Whether you accept it or not, no matter how coveted you try to keep your children, they will experience heartaches, hurt, jealousy, and guilt. Feeling emotions is a certainty no one can escape from. Despite trying to omit and avoid circumstances that are tough and challenging, they will routinely come in contact with them. Since there is not much to control, there is no point in trying to. What you can do, however, is to acknowledge as to what degree these emotions affect their behavior and actions. You have the power to teach them to control their responses to those feelings and learn to regulate them over time. This will help them grow both emotionally and mentally. Coping strategies help the user recognize what emotions they are feeling and how to better address them. Once they address them, they can cultivate an appropriate response to them.

Teaching coping skills will also help them relate to others better and shape their behavior in different situations. The more expressive and understanding they are of their behavior, the better your relationship with them will be. Instead of acting out in frustration or anger, they will express them in manners that are suitable and apposite.

So, how can we teach them and, more importantly, what should we be teaching them? Let's learn together.

The first thing you need to do is help them give that feeling a name. If they are too young, they may not know what terms like "happy, sad, angry" mean. If they are older and school-going, they might interpret their feelings incorrectly. For instance, they may be feeling guilt but interpret it as sadness. As a parent, it is your job to help them identify the feelings and the best way to do so is by labeling it.

The next thing you need to do is identify triggers. What causes a certain feeling? What makes them react in a certain way? Your children should know about the cause and effect reaction. They must be sound enough to identify the things that trigger a certain behavior so they can avoid being in those situations or face them with enhanced confidence.

Tell them it is alright and there is no need to lash out uncontrollably. Often small kids take to throwing tantrums and whining when told "no." When that happens, you have to empathize with them and tell them that what they are experiencing is normal and that you would have been frustrated too if that were to happen to you. However, the goal should be to teach them the right and wrong way of expression. If they are going through something, they should willingly learn to manage it on their own. This develops a sense of independence in them. Let them know they must be cautious of their reactions and words irrespective of the situation.

Once they understand, introduce them to some basic strategies to cope with the emotions they are feeling. For example, if they are feeling down about something, offer some distracting ideas that would uplift their mood. Perhaps suggesting things like going to the park or for a drive or calling up their friend or favorite cousin to cheer up are all great ideas to cope.

Next, don't make the mistake of trying to fix things for them. All children must be encouraged to learn to work through their things independently. We know you hate seeing them sad and know that with a flick of a hand, you can make things better for them. But don't. This is necessary for two reasons: a) they are growing older and less dependent on you and after some time, you won't be able to manipulate the world for them and b) you have to make them learn to cope with uncertainty and unpredictability because, let's face it, life isn't always fair.

And finally, teach them to regulate their emotions using calming techniques so they don't lose their mind over something trivial. Introduce some deep breathing techniques so they can learn to control the urge to react immediately and without thinking straight. Ask them to breathe in and breathe out and make sure to hold their breath for a good 2 to 5 seconds before exhaling the air. Repeat this up to 10 times or more until they calm down and have a grasp on themselves.

If they are continuously distracted by upsetting thoughts like the ones we used to get before the teacher announced the final year results, tell them to start counting. This works well for everyone, even in the time of crisis. If they are in the car, ask them to count how many cars take over; if they are in the playground or social event, ask them to count how many people are wearing a certain color; if they are in the house, ask them to roam around and see how many paintings or frames are hung up in the house.

You can DIY a calming-kit containing their favorite snacks, leisure activity, or books they like to read. It can be crayons and a coloring book, paints, a favorite lotion or perfume, a car set, or soothing tunes they enjoy listening to. All these will not only cheer them up but also allow them to learn that every negative emotion can be turned into something positive.

Tell them they can ask for a time-out or small break if they aren't feeling too well. This could be a minute or 10 to recollect and gather their thoughts before they turn to anxiety and panic. During this time, tell your child to calm down, have a sip of water, and take deep breaths.

Chapter 5: Time to Toughen Up!

Enough talk about it already; in this chapter, we are going to dive straight into the techniques and strategies that will enable you to raise your kids as resilient, confident, self-disciplined, and self-reliant adults. Most of these strategies are backed by years of experiments and research studies, which are a testament of how productive they are.

Try Strength-Based Parenting

According to Lea Waters, a professor at the University of Melbourne, strength-based parenting focuses on the identification and cultivation of positive states, qualities of your child, and processes they go through when faced with a certain situation. Think of it as an addition of a positive filter on parenting that aids parents in teaching kids how to react to stress. This eliminates the chance(s) of kids using aggressive coping reactions or complete avoidance to run away from a stressful situation.

During a preliminary study, Walter and her colleagues explored this newfound concept with a group of primary-school-age children in Australia's middle schools (Waters, 2015). The participating kids were presented with a stressful scenario such as breaking up with a friend over some small fight or being the only student in the class to not have completed an assignment due the next day. The kids are asked to discuss their responses. The majority of the kids came up with negative responses such as freaking out, being depressed, or getting angry. Only a handful of them listed some positive means to cope with the proposed situation. They came up with responses like breathing techniques to get over something faster and reminding themselves of all the good times they had spent with that friend. They also indicated their parents appreciated their strengths and encouraged them to use these kinds of techniques in times of stress to deal with it better.

This suggests that parents who focus more on the skills and strengths of their children rather than pulling them down for their weaknesses are also those who teach them to cope better with stress.

Problem-Solve With Them

Not many parents are aware of the fact that their words hold immense value in the way kids express themselves. If they are reluctant and less open to communication, their kids will refrain from coming to them to discuss how they are feeling. As a result, they may take up unhealthy coping strategies and cause further harm to themselves in the future. Therefore, be communicative and offer problem-solving ideas. Encourage them to think of ways to overcome a certain situation or challenge instead of telling them what to do exactly. Some responses can be:

- What do you think we should do right now?

- Can you tell me how I can make you feel better right now?
- When you faced a similar situation before, what worked for you?
- Can you fill me in with what is going inside your head?
- What can you do to get out of this mess?

Notice how none of these statements offers solutions but rather encourage your kid to come up with one on their own.

Introduce Self-Discipline

Remember the ever-so-famous marshmallow effect? Here's a little reminder if you aren't able to recall the years old test for delayed gratification and self-discipline. Psychologist Walter Mischel called in a few kindergarteners for a test that involved marshmallows. In front of them, each child had a plate containing one marshmallow. The researcher was then called in by someone (planned) but before leaving the room, the researcher made a simple request. If the child wants, they can have the marshmallow right away, but if they waited for the researcher to come back, they will have two. The request was simple but portrayed something very deep within us. It showed how we all are prisoners of instant gratification. Many kids ate the marshmallow without waiting for the researcher. But those who didn't and showed remarkable self-discipline even at such an early age went on to have greater academic scores, better careers, and healthier relationships than their counterparts.

Coming back to the point, every parent must teach their children principles of self-discipline, so they learn to behave appropriately, even when overwhelmed by emotions. The best way to teach a kid that is to make them understand the perks of distraction from temptations. Surely, you may feel like crying a river in the supermarket because the store is out of your favorite gummy bears, but you have to behave and act better. This also builds resilience.

Allow Them to Take Calculated Risks

Be clear when telling them their courage and willingness to fight back and manage emotions is far more commendable than the outcome they achieve. Help them find their freedom to make choices and take decisions so even when they make mistakes, they have no one to blame but themselves. We already established in earlier chapters how this benefits them in the long run. Freedom will facilitate them in knowing what their triggers are, how they can navigate their emotions better, and how to cope with the things that aren't in one's control. They should always be encouraged to take risks and try new things so when they fail, they can learn to get over it and move on. If they won't try anything new, they will spend their whole life in a predictable manner and lose their calm the minute something odd happens. Therefore, it is better to prepare them for uncertainty beforehand.

Avoid Shielding Them From Stress

According to Dennis Charney, a psychiatrist at the Icahn School of Medicine, children who have been through some traumatic experience in their life such as the loss of a parent or loved one, suffered domestic assault, been hit by some natural disaster or been jailed, do better than those who hasn't been through something like that. They portray improved coping skills in difficult times as opposed to those who have had things handed to them with ease.

She explained why such kids are better at bouncing back and healing faster. She believes that since kids who have been through some traumatic incidents have faced challenges right in their faces instead of avoiding their existence or reality, they emerged stronger. For parents, this means engaging kids in challenging tasks, so they learn to cope better and make sense of what is happening instead of running in the other direction. But don't get us wrong, this doesn't mean leaving them in a forest to find their way back home or in an empty parking lot. It is about exposing them to controlled stressful situations that makes them come up with a plan to get out of them. When kids are left on their own to deal with their problems, they develop a psychological toolbox of coping strategies that come in handy when they are adults.

Foster Optimism

Research suggests that optimism is one of the chief traits of resilient people (Ong, et al., 2006). They see the grass greener on both sides, know that the glass is filled (not half-filled or half-empty), and live with a positive outlook towards life. Optimism kills stress and we don't need to provide you with facts to convince you. Therefore, as parents, you must try to nurture optimism by exposing your kids to experiences that make them happier. This doesn't mean you go on invalidating the way they feel but rather presenting them with opportunities that makes them see life as beautiful and worthy. To help them cope with an existing emotion, try to find something positive in it. For example, if your child had been planning for weeks for a school trip and for some reason it got canceled at the last minute, take them someplace they enjoy going to so they understand that all is never lost.

The idea is to refocus their attention on what is left from what has been lost.

Increase Social Interactions

Social support is another great way to build resilience and grit in children. When kids are surrounded by people who admire them, encourage them and support them through thick and thin, they feel loved and looked after. Social support has been linked to positive emotions, predictability of behavior, and improved self-esteem, motivation, and personal control. Name the ones who always cheer them on when they are faced with difficult emotions. Strong connections with people who love them also make them resilient.

Tell Them It Is Okay to Seek Help

Being brave doesn't always mean dealing with things alone. It also means you can seek assistance when required without feeling ashamed or guilty. After all, two minds are always better than one, so remind them to seek help and not carry all the burdens alone.

Let Them Heal

Often, we presume that resilience is about never failing. But it is about getting back up, recovering, and gaining back control of your life. A lot of times, parents try to rush through an array of emotions, hoping the sooner their system is flushed off them the better. But like any injury, a broken or hurt person needs time to heal. There is a reason why we feel things so deeply. We can't push them away or get over them in a minute. This is deceit and denial, and sooner or later, they will crawl back into our minds and do the damage. The healing time is when one reviews the problem, reflects upon and processes mistakes, and finds means to restore balance. Rushing through emotions doesn't build resilience; embracing and acknowledging them does!

Conclusion

Whenever we are faced with fear, uncertainty, or anxiety and don't respond in a resilient manner, we pass it on to our kids too. As parents, we are always over-directing and overprotecting our kids. We are the sole reason why they turn into risk-averse rule-followers. But these aren't the skills that will help them survive what's out there; their curiosity, adaptability, flexibility, and risk-taking will. This is the mindset that makes them resilient and strong in times of hardships and troubles and allows them to cope with the challenges and failures as they come.

From an early age, we have been rewarding them for memorizing and cramming the right answers. But what we don't realize is their inquisitiveness will be pivotal. Why? Because thanks to technology, they are able to seek answers to god knows whatever comes to their mind with a swipe of their finger in less than 10 seconds. However, once they have the answer, how they use it, process it, evaluate it, and stitch it together is what matters more – again, something that has less to do with cramming and more with how smart and creative they are.

As they grow older and reach their teen years, we force them to compete for trophies, a few slots in a top university, and indirectly preach insensitivity towards others. What we need to teach them instead is collaboration and how they can work flexibly with all types of people in perfect harmony and learn to be responsible for their actions. Tomorrow's world is less about competition and more about collaboration.

What we need to do is teach them to become resilient so that whatever circumstances they have to face, they are mentally and emotionally-prepared to handle them.

In this guide, we hope we have lived up to the promise we started with – to help you prepare your child for the tough and competitive world outside. If we were to do a quick recap of everything that has been covered in this book, it should look something like this – we started off with understanding what resilience means, why our kids need to develop it, and how we can teach them and encourage them using the 7 Cs of building resilience.

In chapter two, we talked about how parents can cultivate and foster creativity in kids and believe and hone their skills and talents to nurture them. We also learned of the importance of discipline and how parents can use empathy to teach rather than use punishment to make them resilient.

In the following chapter, we learned how we can teach children to own up to their mistakes and what role can parents play to correct wrong behavior and approaches using effective strategies.

In chapter four, we saw how we can help kids navigate their way through stress and other negative emotions. We talked about the importance of developing coping skills and presented reader parents with some great ones to get started with.

In the final chapter of the book, we looked at how we can put all the knowledge we have gained into practice. This is, by far, the most crucial step of the entire book. We looked at multiple research studies and tried to understand their links with resilience.

Use this as a guide to better parenting. Identify the things you can work upon and introduce practices that will help your child grow up to become resilient, independent, and ready for the world!

References

7 C's of resilience. (2017, April 4). Retrieved from https://activeforlife.com/7-cs-of-resilience/

Ackerman, C. E. (2019, October 4). What is Resilience and Why is It Important to Bounce Back? Retrieved from https://positivepsychology.com/what-is-resilience/

Barker, E. (2014, March 24). How to Raise Happy Kids: 10 Steps Backed by Science. Retrieved from https://time.com/35496/how-to-raise-happy-kids-10-steps-backed-by-science/

Carter, C. (n.d.). 7 Ways to Foster Creativity in Your Kids. Retrieved from https://greatergood.berkeley.edu/article/item/7_ways_to_foster_creativity_in_your_kids

Gottfredson, L. S. (1996). What Do We Know About Intelligence? i, 15-30.

Hogg, E. (2016, October 24). How to discipline kids: Punishment is OUT, Empathy is IN. Retrieved from https://www.fitmaltamums.com/how-to-discipline-kids-punishment-is-out-empathy-is-in/

Hyman, S. M., & Sinha, R. (2008). Stress-Related Factors in Cannabis Use and Misuse: Implications for Prevention and Treatment. Journal of Substance Abuse Treatment, 400–413.

Jones, D. E., Greenberg, M., & Crowley, M. (2015). Early Social-Emotional Functioning and Public Health: The Relationship Between Kindergarten Social Competence and Future Wellness. American Journal of Public Health, 2283–2290.

Kidtelligent. (n.d.). Retrieved from http://blog.kidtelligent.com/10-ways-to-teach-children-to-accept-their-mistakes/

Learning from Mistakes: Why We Need to Let Children Fail. (n.d.). Retrieved from https://www.brighthorizons.com/family-resources/the-importance-of-mistakes-helping-children-learn-from-failure

Markham, L. (2018, October 11). Don't set your child up for extra frustration. Retrieved from https://www.mother.ly/child/how-to-raise-kids-resilience?rebelltitem=11#rebelltitem11

Ong, A. D., Toni, B. L., Wallace, K. A., & Bergeman, C. S. (2006). Psychological resilience, positive emotions, and successful adaptation to stress in later life. Journal of Personality and Social Psychology, 730–749.

Oosthuizen, R. M. (2020). Resilience to Emotional Distress in Response to Failure, Error or Mistakes: A Positive Psychology Review. Springer, 237-258.

Reznick, C. (2009). The Power of Your Child's Imagination: How to Transform Stress and Anxiety into Joy and Success. New York: TarcherPerigee.

Rubin, K. H., Coplan, R. J., & Bowker, J. C. (2009). Social withdrawal in childhood. Annual Review of Psychology, 141-171.

Sharma, M. (2016, July 15). 5 Reasons Why You Should Never Compare Your Kids with Others. Retrieved from https://www.huffingtonpost.in/meha-sharma/five-reasons-why-we-shoul_b_8660618.html

Solomons, K. (2013). Born to be Worthless: The Hidden Power of Low Self-Esteem. North Charleston: CreateSpace Independent Publishing Platform.

Waters, L. (2015). The Relationship between Strength-Based Parenting with Children's Stress Levels and Strength-Based Coping Approaches. Psychology, 689-699.

What does resilience really mean? (2010, February 20). Retrieved from https://www.diploweb.com/What-does-resilience-really-mean.html

Young, E. (2019, November 5). Five Ways to Boost Resilience in Children. Retrieved from https://digest.bps.org.uk/2019/11/05/five-ways-to-boost-resilience-in-children/

Young, K. (2018, August 30). 20 Powerful Strategies in Building Resilience in Children. Retrieved from https://www.heysigmund.com/building-resilience-children/

HOW PARENTS CAN TEACH CHILDREN TO COUNTER NEGATIVE THOUGHTS

Channelling Your Child's Negativity, Self-Doubt, and Anxiety into Resilience, Willpower, and Determination

FRANK DIXON

© **Copyright 2020 - All rights reserved.**

The content contained within this book may not be reproduced, duplicated or transmitted without direct written permission from the author or the publisher.

Under no circumstances will any blame or legal responsibility be held against the publisher, or author, for any damages, reparation, or monetary loss due to the information contained within this book, either directly or indirectly.

Legal Notice:

This book is copyright protected. It is only for personal use. You cannot amend, distribute, sell, use, quote or paraphrase any part, or the content within this book, without the consent of the author or publisher.

Disclaimer Notice:

Please note the information contained within this document is for educational and entertainment purposes only. All effort has been executed to present accurate, up to date, reliable, complete information. No warranties of any kind are declared or implied. Readers acknowledge that the author is not engaged in the rendering of legal, financial, medical or professional advice. The content within this book has been derived from various sources. Please consult a licensed professional before attempting any techniques outlined in this book.

By reading this document, the reader agrees that under no circumstances is the author responsible for any losses, direct or indirect, that are incurred as a result of the use of the information contained within this document, including, but not limited to, errors, omissions, or inaccuracies.

Introduction

Hey, you!

Are you up for some story time? Well, here's one you are going to remember for a long, long time!

It was the 1980s. In a school in Tennessee, one of the teachers, while teaching a class complained of something smelling "gasoline-like." As soon as she made that claim, she started to get sick. She felt short of breath, had nausea, a headache and also reported dizziness. Almost everyone in her class started to exhibit the same symptoms and before you know it, the whole school was stricken.

Firefighters were called upon to the scene and the school was evacuated. The police and ambulances also arrived and by evening, some 80 students and 19 teachers and staff members were admitted to the local emergency room, of which, 38 stayed overnight at the hospital.

After several inspections at the school and investigations by Government agencies, the authorities were unable to find any traces of gas leaks. The blood reports of the admitted patients didn't show any toxic substances or gases in their system. As it turns out, the fear of "being poisoned" had fueled the symptoms in the kids and staff members.

According to one of the epidemiologists, the outbreak was due to a phenomenon we now come to know as mass psychogenic illness. This happens when the fear of infection is as deadly as the disease itself and tricks the brain into thinking that the disease has been acquired and thus, it starts to show symptoms commonly associated with it. The students too had perceived that there was some threat plaguing them and thus started to show similar symptoms.

This tells us two things. First, our mind is a remarkable and stupid thing. On one end, it allows us to explore so much in the universe, store and process so much information at once and yet, sometimes, so stupid to get tricked in this way. Second, it shows us the power of fear and negative thinking and what it can do to the human brain.

Fear–as old as humans themselves–is a deeply wired reaction that allows us to protect ourselves against threats and dangers. It is what kept the cavemen alive for many years without forming tribes, and it still grips us by the throat when something unexpected comes our way. And believe it or not, we revere it. If we didn't, we wouldn't have dedicated a whole day of celebration to it.

It is fear that breeds negative thoughts–not just in adults but also in kids. Negative thoughts are the worst enemy of a bright and creative mind. Most kids are intrinsically artistic and creative. They have congenital confidence that they are the rulers of the world. Everyone around them is always wanting them to have the best, look the best, and eat the best. Don't we, as parents, have the same? We want them to have the best of both worlds, fulfill their lifelong dreams, live up to set expectations, and follow their dreams without an ounce of self-doubt and fear in the minds.

But what can we do to ensure that they get all of the things mentioned without losing their confidence or giving in to negative thoughts? In this book, we are going to help parents guide and prepare their children for a better and confident tomorrow. We want parents to be able to teach their children resilience, the power of self-discipline, and determination. We want parents to nurture confidence, strong-mindedness, and emotional intelligence in them so that they can counter and whitewash negative thinking from the core.

Chapter 1: Into the Child's Mind

A child's brain is an amazing thing. It is like a whole universe, just waiting to be explored and discovered. Did you know, until the last decade, scientists and researchers believed that children were just miniature versions of adults? They, for the longest time, believed that their minds functioned in the same manner as that of an adult and it is only a matter of time that they learned new skills and practiced their skills. But since this belief doesn't hold true, we see children depicting behaviors we wouldn't observe in an adult. Things like crying over something insignificant or holding onto grudges. Although adults might do something similar, they have a way of convincing themselves of the other positive things out there. Kids, not so much. If they are fixated on something, well that's it then.

Granted, there is nothing wrong with having a strong and determined mind from an early age. However, it can become a problem if that mind is determined to host negative thoughts. Negative thoughts like body-image issues, lack of confidence, low self-esteem, etc., are things that breed negativity on a larger scale. When not discouraged from having such thoughts or paying heed to them, it can land kids in unthinkable troubles in academia, social, and their future professional lives. When they keep submitting to negativity, they rarely focus on the good and thus, lead a life full of disappointments, heartbreaks, and mental health issues.

Even in our wildest dreams, we wouldn't want to raise kids as such. So in this first chapter, we are going to be looking at what negative thoughts are, their types, and then explore why some kids find it so easy to just give up.

What Are Negative Thoughts?

Negative thinking is a whirlpool of thoughts that leads to people finding the worst in everything. It also means these people might reduce their expectations so low that their minds only come up with the worst-case scenarios. It is like a web, each thought connected with newer thoughts developing every second. Imagine this: your child has been asked to play a small role in a school play. It is a small part with almost zero dialogue. All your child has to do is stand on one side, wearing the costume of a tree. Your child is naturally shy and thinks that they will not be able to pull it off.

"Can you tell Ms. Nora that I won't be able to perform in the play?"

"But why?"

"I don't think I can do it. What if I make a fool out of myself? What if I vomit or faint on the stage? Everyone will laugh at me. They will call me a loser

forever. I will have no friends and no one will ever forget it."

Notice how the child is thinking the worst and how each thought is just a continuation of the previous one like a vicious thread? This is what negative thinking looks like. It shatters a child's confidence and makes them believe that they are good for nothing. It can manifest in a pattern of worry, stress, and depression over time.

Many kids are prone to negative thinking. It is what leads them to have meltdowns, engage in fights, and make risky decisions. When they are young, they aren't able to comprehend the many thoughts in their head but as they grow older and reach early adolescence, they begin to associate connections. For instance, they learn that a normal behavior to exhibit when sad is crying. They learn that sometimes when they are anxious or stressed, they turn to bite their nails or pace back and forth in a room. These are all natural reactions to stressful or disturbing situations. However, a reaction is different from behavior. While the former is more natural, the latter isn't. It is more of a choice. How we choose to behave, address, and process what is going on is what we refer to as our 'behavior.'

To teach any behavior, it has to be repeated enough times that it turns into a habit–something you do unintentionally, like putting your hand on your mouth when yawning, or closing your eyes when faced with danger or horror.

Therefore, as parents, we need to instill such habits in our kids that will automatically help them to navigate their way to positivity and optimism.

Negative thinking works on two principles:

1. It disqualifies the positive. Meaning, it dismisses any positive thought or acknowledgment in our head and takes us back to thinking illogically. We only see the negatives with clarity.

2. It maximizes the negative and minimizes the positive. So instead of looking at our positive achievements, we magnify our losses and failures, even if they are small.

There are many different ways of how negativity can manifest itself. It mostly comes in one or more of the following forms.

- Cynicism: This is the most common and usually denotes that your child has a general distrust for people. They have a difficult time listening to people who are trying to encourage them and doubt their motives instead.

- Hostility: Hostility is usually prominent in adolescents and teenagers. As their bodies grow, the chemical imbalances and hormonal changes often lead to mood swings. They develop feelings of unfriendliness towards others and become hesitant in opening up or developing new relationships.

- Polarized Thinking: This way of thinking usually suggests that if a child thinks they are not good at something, say playing the piano or math, then they think they are horrible. They don't believe in being average and don't make any effort to become better at it. It's black or white for them.

- Filtering: This is rather self-explanatory. Kids only notice the bad—or worse—they magnify it in their minds.

- Jump to Conclusions: Some children are quick to assume the worst in things. If something remotely scary comes their way, they take no time in thinking about the worst-case scenarios. They think nothing good can come out of a bad situation ever.

- Blaming: Kids with negativity corrupting their minds also find it easier to blame others for their own maladies. They often take the role of the victim in everything, thinking nothing fair ever happens to them.

- Heaven's Reward Fallacy: They are staunch believers that if they work hard or sacrifice, they will be rewarded. However, when that reward doesn't come, they take to depression and bitterness. An example of this looks something like this: your child studies hard for exams and pulls all-nighters. However, when the result is out, they don't score well. So the next time, they don't work hard at all.

Why It's Easy to Just Give Up

Giving up is sometimes the easiest thing to do. As adults, we are ourselves guilty of this habit, so we don't get to simply tell our kids not to. Many people, children included, give up because they can't face the stress and pain associated with something and they'd rather put an end to the misery. We choose not to endanger our comfort and step out to make sacrifices, all for some uncertain future. Doesn't seem like a very wise bargain, does it?

But do you know why we must always bet against the odds? It is because there is one thing more damaging and hurtful and that is regret. If you don't try, regret will always follow. If you don't encourage your kids to try and never quit, then they will always regret it later. It is an unwanted feeling that keeps us stuck in the past. Had I chosen to take that course during my semester break, I would have been promoted. Had I learned a unique skill, it would have helped me get the job. Had I chosen to follow my passion for sports, I could have made a blooming career out of it.

We don't want our children to live with regrets. Let's say, they are giving up something because the goal doesn't seem appealing. Let's say it is revising everything that has been taught at school. They say that it is too tiring and time-consuming and they would rather spend their time playing outdoors or on a game on their tablet. They promise you that they will start studying once the finals are near and make it up.

For the following days, they will feel relieved that they don't have to do it anymore. Might even enjoy the free time for a few weeks, but then what? They will have regrets a few months later when they have to study for the finals and spend hours in their room, sunken in their books. Not to mention, the additional stress and pressure of learning about so much in such a short period. That is when the regret will settle in and make them panic. That is when they will start to hate themselves and a little bit of you too, for not pushing them hard enough to stick with the studying. Not only that, but they also will not be able to perform their best and pass the class with decent grades.

There are several reasons why kids find giving up easy. Let's discuss a few.

They don't have a strong 'Why?'

Did you know, Walt Disney was fired several times and told that he had no original ideas and lacked imagination? Had he chosen to give up, we wouldn't have the world of Disney and the amazing shows we grew up watching.

Like Mr. Walt, some kids don't have a compelling reason to keep going. They lack the answer to that 'why' that our brain keeps asking us as we work towards a goal. When the answer isn't powerful enough, we are likely to give up.

Expecting Fast Results

Some kids, although not suffering from ADHD, just want things to move at a fast pace. They want quick results and are rarely willing to do the work when it comes to something detail-oriented. They are also the ones who resort to taking shortcuts. Shortcuts work, no doubt about that, but not always. And when things don't go as planned, meltdowns and frustration are bound to happen.

As parents, we have to make them patient and have a more stable and calm mindset. We must let them know that not all goals can be achieved in a short period and thus, they must continue to work for them without getting disheartened. Some may have gotten it easy and have things presented to them on a silver plate, but life isn't fair to all and that is okay. A classic example of this can be your teenager trying to lose weight to look a certain way but wanting quick results. So, they resort to quick fixes and aren't willing to do the actual work. They starve themselves, boycott all carbs and later, complain of dizziness and poor concentration and energy levels.

Presuming They Have Unique Problems

A lot of kids presume that no one will understand what they are going through because their problems are so unique. Oh, really? Are you the first-ever child to be bullied at school? Are you the first-ever human to have been compared to an older sibling or cousin? Are you the first-ever individual to have broken up with a friend or a partner?

Kids who assume they have unique problems fail to see the larger picture. They think that what they are going through is something their parents, peers, or friends won't understand. So, they bother not to speak about them or find solutions.

Doubting Capabilities

Some kids just don't find that push within themselves to bring ideas to fruition. It isn't that they aren't smart, they just lack confidence and believe that they will be ridiculed or made fun of. A lack of confidence in our abilities often halts us from trying new things. Many kids, doubting their skills and abilities abandon their long-term goals. Here's the thing: if you don't have the right mindset and you are always listening to your inner critic, you will be pushing away a lot of valuable things in life. Therefore, we parents have to ensure that our kids don't feel discouraged and fail to fulfill their dreams and aspirations. We have to be their encouragement and that push that makes them want to see what's at the bottom of the cliff and later, dive their way through the crest and trough of life. We have to remind them how wholesome it can feel to achieve their goals and make them experience the joy that comes with it.

One Failure Wears Them Down

Why are kids so quick to give up, you ask? They think that if they are putting their heart and soul into something, it should come out right. Be it a school project, an assignment, or an exam. However, one failure is enough to get them off track and concoct negative thoughts. Failure too can be rewarding. You learn from your mistakes and rethink strategies from a different angle. It piques curiosity and can also serve as a motivation to try harder. Besides, achieving something isn't always on the cards. For some kids, it comes a little late and for some it never does. In both these cases, as parents, we have to make them see the bright side of things and prevent them from going into self-doubt.

Kids who are quick to give in whenever they come across the first stumbling block can take more time in training and developing positive habits. But, it isn't impossible.

Lack of Self-Discipline and Resilience in Life

Some kids give up easily because they lack the discipline required to stay patient and wait for the rewards. Since they aren't disciplined, they expect quick results. They are soon to judge and give up because, according to them, things haven't turned out the way they had wanted and thus, there really isn't any point further in sticking to working hard. However, this is what the most important lesson is. They must learn to become disciplined and have control over their emotions and feelings.

Chapter 2: What Negativity Does to Your Child?

Do you know who the biggest criticizers of your kids are? Themselves. They can and will do enough damage to themselves if the negative self-talk doesn't stop. We have to teach them how to not let their inner critic prevent them from harm. The reason negative thoughts aren't ever welcoming is that they bring along emotions like anger, frustration, and stress along with them. It may take you hours to convince them why they should look at the positive aspect of things but only a second for their inner critic to change their mind about it. The only way we can stop them is by identifying negative or harmful behaviors, which means that it has already done some of the fundamental damage. This means that we as parents, have to gear up and teach them how to look past their failures, losses, and have an optimistic mindset.

The Effects of Negativity on Our Mind and Body

During one study, researchers found that negative thinking is linked with an increased risk of developing mental health issues. This means that kids who are brought up in an environment that offers them no opportunities to grow, be positive, and achieve their dreams with determination, are likelier to suffer from mental health issues later in life (Kinderman, Schwannauer, Pontin, & Tai, 2013).

Furthermore, it can have some negative effects on the mind and body.

For instance, it can trigger hopelessness. Kids experience decreased motivation and willpower to continue with something important. They are sure of their loss from the start. This feeling of hopelessness makes an easy task seem hard and combined with a lack of motivation and drive leads to negative thoughts clouding the mind.

Negative thoughts also limit a child's thought process and problem-solving skills. They keep listening to that inner voice that takes immense pleasure in reminding them things they aren't capable of, instead of the ones they are. This limits their thinking to reason creatively and step out of the comfort zone to give something challenging a try.

Kids prone to negative thinking also believe that perfectionism is attainable. Although not entirely accomplishable, perfectionism can be a great booster to help kids aim higher. However, studies suggest that focusing too much on it can lead to increased stress about everything. Think about it this way: your child wishes to impress their new art teacher with a sketch. They want it to be perfect, so they spend more time working on it. However, every time they look at it, the more problems they find in it. So, they keep going back and forth revising and redrawing it.

A perfectionist can never be happy with what they have and tries to keep improving it. It can be quite addictive and stressful, especially for young kids.

Children with a negative outlook about life are also depressed (Schimelpfening, 2020). When left unchecked, little bouts of temporary depression can become quite damaging.

And how can we forget that the biggest and most pressing issue with negative thinking is that it isn't *positive* self-talk? Simplistic as it is, there is tons of research that positive self-talk results in good academia, a successful career, healthier well-being, and meaningful relationships (Tod, Hardy, & Oliver, 2011).

And to provide you with a rather interesting research study involving 400,000 white people and 300,000 Chinese-Americans, researchers in San Diego were astonished to look at the findings.

It all began when some researchers looked at the death records of the said amount of randomly-selected white people and Chinese Americans (Philips, Ruth & Wagner, 1993). They found that Chinese Americans died earlier than most white Americans. As it turns out, the Chinese Americans that had a combination of an ill-fated birth year (as per the Chinese astrology and medicine) and disease died five years earlier than the rest.

Researchers further dug into the causes of their deaths and concluded that the more strongly the

Chinese Americans believed in the Chinese superstitions about the ill-fated birth year, the sooner they died. The reduction in their life expectancy wasn't explainable by genetic factors, their behavior, lifestyle choices, or the skills of the doctors treating their respective diseases.

They were dying younger not due to the disease or their flawed genes but due to their strong negative beliefs. They believed that since the stars had hexed them, they were doomed to die earlier. It was nothing but their negative attitude towards life that led them to their ultimate deaths. Quite literally!

What we must notice here is the strong connection between the human brain and body. Negative emotions and stress are becoming two of the most important causes of diseases worldwide. The negativity leads to chronic stress which weakens the heart and impairs the functioning of other organs such as the lungs, kidneys, and liver. When the body is under constant stress, the body loses its balance. It becomes harder to digest and takes more time for us to heal. This makes resting difficult and the lack of rest and sleep brings more problems to the table.

Putting an End to It for Good

How can we, as parents, help our young people break this cycle of negativity and stop paying attention to that inner critic?

We, being the role models and idols they look up to, can contribute in more than one way or another to help them in this tough time. But as they say, practice what you preach, it has to start with you. If your child looks up to a parent who is always nagging about the lack of things, blaming others for their problems, and treating every new opportunity as an obstacle or challenge, they are going to pick up the same. If they see you complaining, they will complain too. If they see you being negative, they will have a negative outlook on things too. If they see you giving up your dreams because of the fear of failure or "what others will say," then they won't have the guts to try something new either. So to change them, you have to change yourself first. You will have to embrace positivity and optimism because that is how healthy habits take form. Whether you accept it or not, they are going to take after you and take up habits they see you practicing. So be the right kind of role model for your kids first and *then* preach about the power of positive thinking.

Say Positive Things to Them

As a parent, you have to help them see the positive in everything–especially when they fail at something. You have to point out the good in every circumstance whether they like it or not. The idea is to get them thinking if the outcome can be positive in some way or not. Once they start to give positive thinking a chance, it will become easier for them in the long-run. Ideally, you should radiate positivity. It allows children to see that there is another, more promising way of looking at things that don't end with frustration and sadness.

Teach Them About the Monkey Mind

Monkey Mind is an approach to view and process things. It originates from the Zen concept and suggests that since our brain works tirelessly all day long, transitions from one idea to another, listens to endless chatter both from the internal and external world, craves things, and becomes judgmental, it is very easy to get confused. So much happens in the mind that it leaves the little one confused as to what to listen to what thoughts to discard. The brain of a monkey functions in the same manner, says Dr. Arnold who introduced the concept to the world. He goes on to suggest that negative thoughts are like a monkey, climbing from one tree to another. This hinders focus on important tasks. For instance, when kids want to focus on some tasks at hand, they often get distracted. Things like procrastination, lack of focus, external distractions like noise, chatter, and people around make it harder to concentrate. All these things when amalgamated leads to negative thinking. First, procrastination delays the process, then a lack of focus makes simple tasks appear difficult, next external noises and chatter just add more pressure on the kids. Thus, they give up the task altogether.

So how to stop the monkey from climbing one tree after another and giving up everything important because it seems hard?

Dr. Arnold believes that to flip negative thinking, we must direct kids to follow these three steps.

1. Take a deep breath.
2. Tell yourself to "stop and relax" sternly.
3. And chant something positive to yourself like, "I got this" or "I can handle it."

This simple exercise can help kids break the chain of negative thoughts and replace them with something positive.

Keep a Gratitude Journal

Gratitude journals or simply listing down five things you are grateful for in life is a great way to keep the mind focused on the positives in our lives. Make it a routine to encourage the habit of keeping a gratitude journal or reminding your kids to count their blessings before going to bed so that it is the last thing they remember and wake up feeling positive and motivated.

If they aren't too keen on maintaining a gratitude journal, simply ask them to write their thoughts in a diary. The idea is to offer them a vessel to pour in their feelings. Haven't we all felt a whole lot better after discussing our problems and worries with someone? However, since most kids feel shy about taking their problems to their parents, this can work in their favor and prevent the frustration and negative thinking that builds up inside them. When they are made to feel grateful for the things they have, it changes the way they think and views things. They start to approach things with a new sense of positivity and with elevated motivation.

Problem-Solve With Them

Keep in mind there is a big difference between problem-solving with them and for them. You have to help them come up with solutions or lead them with hints on how to do things so that they don't give up on them easily. For instance, if they are doing a puzzle, you can guide them by asking them to try putting a certain piece to check if it fits or not. The idea is to help them but make them think that they came up with it on their own. Not only does this encourage them to keep attempting and trying, but it also instills a sense of victory in them. It makes them feel confident in their abilities and with time, makes them self-reliant.

Empathize

Knowing that others understand what they are going through is another way to lessen the impact of negative thinking. Empathizing with your child allows you to show them that feeling a certain way is completely normal. It makes them feel heard and understood. When kids feel heard and cared for, they feel more supported and become more willing to give things another try in case they didn't work out the first time. For instance, saying things like, "I know you must be feeling like a complete failure to not have caught that ball in the game, but you aren't one. You will catch it the next time," can be motivating.

Switch Perspectives

"What would your favorite athlete or celebrity do if they were in this rut?"

Teaching kids to think from someone else's perspective gives their problems a new meaning and visualization. For example, if they are a fan of some rock star or footballer, ask them what they would have done in this situation. Not only does that offer some form of positive distraction, but it also helps kids try to come up with solutions on their own. After all, they wouldn't want to disappoint their favorite character. If they still seem unconvinced, ask them if their favorite rock star would have said, "I Quit" too?

Chapter 3: Am I Good Enough?

Another issue prevalent among kids is a lack of confidence. They suffer from low self-esteem and think that they aren't good enough. They rarely hone their skills and natural talents because they think there is no point to it. They often act shy and avoid social interactions, which prevents them from developing meaningful and deep connections. They feel reluctant in signing up for something new or accepting opportunities that knock on their doors. They often report feeling unloved and unwanted. You can often see them expressing negativity as they feel they are the victims of other's devilish plans. They are quick to blame others for their mistakes and don't have the strength to own up to them. When they feel frustrated, they don't know how to handle it, which means their emotional intelligence is suffering too. They are always comparing themselves with others above them and not with the ones less privileged than them. They hesitate to build new relationships due to fear of rejection and embarrassment. They also suffer from low bouts of motivation and don't take encouraging compliments well.

Noticing these signs in your little one can be heartbreaking and worrying for parents. No one wants their kids to suffer and every parent wants their child to live their lives in a more wholesome and prosperous manner. Therefore, if you are one of those parents with a kid suffering from a lack of confidence in their abilities and skills, this chapter is especially for you. Here we talk about the dangers and impacts of self-doubt on our children's lives. We see how it hurts them academically, personally, and socially. Later, we discuss the reasons that lead to low self-esteem issues in kids.

The Dangers of Self-Doubt

Our self-esteem is what reflects the way we feel about ourselves and how we approach things. Although every individual has a different level of self-esteem, it is often described as how they see their worth in the world. People who suffer from low self-esteem tend to lead a harder life as they feel incompetent at everything and thus don't approach things wholeheartedly. This means that low self-esteem affects our behavior and mood too. It is also viewable from our body language and overall demeanor towards life.

Therefore, when it comes to our children, we have to model high self-esteem from the beginning. We have to encourage and instill behaviors and habits that make them feel confident and ready. If we don't, here's how life can look for them.

Children who have self-confidence issues are unable to feel comfortable around people. This means that when we choose to not teach them how to be confident, we are depriving them of meaningful and deep relationships. Having no friends or peers to look up to can be damaging to their personality.

These kids also depict avoidance behaviors, which means they are more hesitant to seek challenges or take risks than those who are taught to be confident. They have a hard time stepping out of their comfort zones and thus, fail to grow and experience many important things in life.

They can also be seen talking negatively about themselves and their abilities. They are highly critical of their appearances and talents. You can expect them to have slumped shoulders, an overall sad expression on their faces, and downcast eyes, says Joe Navarro, a former FBI counterintelligence agent during an interview with Psychology Today.

A child who suffers from poor levels of confidence also feels unskilled and incompetent when it comes to completing tasks. They are ready to give up the minute something goes against their plans and walk away. In contrast, someone with better confidence will keep on trying until they get it right and not fear failure, loss, or embarrassment.

Lastly, all these inabilities lead to a negative outlook on life. They become pessimistic and in case you didn't notice it in the earlier chapter, it can be really hard to let go of that.

What Funnels Self-Esteem Issues in Kids?

How children feel about themselves is a consequence of the things they have experienced. We all are, in fact, the product of what we experience as our experiences are what changes us–for either the good or bad. How we deal with them determines our attitude. In adolescents and teenagers, these are the following causes of poor self-esteem.

Encouragement and Support Shortfall

The foremost reason why some kids suffer from low self-esteem is that they don't feel supported or encouraged by their loved ones. These include their parents, friends, relatives, and peers. When kids don't receive adequate encouragement, they begin to internalize that they aren't good enough or wanted.

Criticism

If a child is frequently criticized for their mistakes, they start to step back from trying things and suffer from low self-confidence. Criticism from parents should come in a way that it doesn't feel humiliating or sarcastic. It should be aimed to improve and enhance their skills rather than demotivate or degrade them. The result could be a child thinking themselves incapable and incompetent.

Stressful Life Events

Have the parents recently divorced or has the family moved homes? Stressful events as such can also leave a long-lasting negative impression on a child's mind. They feel the stress is too big and find it difficult to cope.

Trauma or Abuse

When a child has been through some trauma like an accident, the loss of a parent, or from abuse (mental, emotional or physical), they begin to suffer from low self-esteem. They think that nothing good will ever happen to them and feel like they have been truly cursed. So they basically just give up on life and all that it has to offer, thinking, "what's the point, anyways."

Bullying

Being bullied, either at school, among friends or at home can also hurt a child's self-esteem. They shouldn't be made to feel like they aren't worthy of the good things or are just a nuisance in the lives of others. This can trigger isolation and social distancing, which leads to loneliness and depression as they grow older.

Negative Comparisons

Do you often compare your kids with your friends' kids or with their friends? You want them to be like them, which sounds like a good idea to you, but it isn't. Kids who feel like they have to live up to someone else to be considered intelligent or smart also suffer from low self-esteem. Basically, when we tell them to be like someone else, we are really telling them to give up on who they are and change. This too can foster negativity in them and they may forever feel inept.

Unrealistic Expectations

Setting unachievable goals in life is another way to inflict low self-esteem in kids. The pressure to be a certain someone can come from parents, peers, teachers, or friends. Imposing unrealistic expectations means that they will constantly struggle to meet them and probably fail. The failure ensures that they were indeed right about their poor skills and abilities.

Chapter 4: I Am Confident and Self-Reliant

Confidence comes from positive outcomes. Positive outcomes fuel confidence as they serve as motivators. When we put our heart and soul into something, say like a new recipe, and it turns out amazing and bags us compliments from our spouse and kids, don't we feel confident? Doesn't that give us the motivation to try something new the next day?

It helps kids improve in the same manner too. When something they did reaps positive outcomes, they feel more confident and self-reliant. When they feel confident and assured, they feel empowered to invest their time and resources in other things too. Confidence is what makes kids persistent. Without, we give up soon or simply don't start at all. So in a way, we can say that it is what saves kids from despair and hopelessness.

The Barriers to Self-Confidence in Kids

However, there are some barriers when encouraging kids to be self-confident. Before we head straight into teaching you strategies to help empower your kids to become confident adults, it is only fair to know of and eliminate the factors that pose hurdles in our efforts.

Self-Defeating Assumptions

Some kids just think that they can't, so they don't try. Sometimes, they become so rattled by a little inconvenience that they call quits to the next one without even a single attempt. They decide to let go of something, assuming they won't be able to have it. For instance, a child may decide to learn to play baseball. However, every time they try to play catch with their older sibling, they miss all catches. So, they decide to not join the school team–assuming they will be bad at it. These are what we call, self-defeating assumptions. It's good to be realistic but that doesn't mean you start to act like a loser before even trying. Kids who believe in such self-defeating assumptions can be hard to train.

Setting Unrealistic Goals

On the contrary, some kids act like big shows and take up more than they could handle. It's ambitious to tackle BHAGs (big hairy audacious goals) but only if you are prepared for it. Enormous goals often undermine confidence. This can stem from demotivation and depression. Confidence is something that mostly comes from small wins at first.

Celebrating Too Soon

Do you have a child who celebrates their weight loss by eating an entire cake? What kind of celebration is it? Kids who claim to be victors before reaching their end goals can trigger a lack of confidence when they fail at the next stage. For instance, your kid scores high grades in math during a class test. So, they confidently announce it to the whole class that they will be one getting the highest grade in math in the finals. Seems the right kind of anticipation, right? But before the finals, they have to score high in the next test too, which they don't. And then there goes their confidence out of the door.

Blaming Others

Kids who don't own up to their mistakes and instead blame others for their mishaps are also hard to train. They, themselves are the barrier to building confidence as they aren't willing to listen and make amends to their behavior and thoughts. Even when wronged by someone, we still have the choice to either cry about it or make a difference for ourselves. Sadly, kids who choose the first often report having poor confidence and show resistance when schooled about it.

Not Anticipating Setbacks

A child who doesn't anticipate setbacks and moves forward with blind optimism may stumble and fall hard on their head. Optimism is a good thing but when it clouds the mind of a child, they forget about the dangers and challenges along the way. Therefore, when something unexpected happens, they lose their confidence and edge. This is the hardest to treat as they have had a taste of positivity before and now have turned bitter and hopeless.

Being Overconfident

There is a fine line between being confident and arrogant and kids who don't understand that, often end up crossing it. Arrogance can lead to neglecting the basics, turning a deaf ear to the critics, and being blinded by the forces of change.

Learning to Shut the Inner Voice

All kids need positive affirmations to defeat the inner critic. As parents, we can help them find that positivity and turn their negative perceptions into something positive and progressive. First off, we must use language that reeks of positivity, even when they feel down. This kind of outlook about everything is what they are going to pick up too and use to uplift their confidence. Other than that:

You must, at all times, love them. This seems rather debatable as every parent thinks they love their child unconditionally. True, but sometimes we forget to show it to them. Love demands actions and actions drive behavior. Dole out plenty of love their way to encourage them and make them realize that they always have a strong support system behind them. This also means putting an end to baseless comparisons and extremely high expectations that they will fail to meet. Every child, including yours, needs to feel accepted and looked after. When we yell, shout, or ignore them, we are unconsciously undermining their level of confidence. Ever had your child come up to you to show you how well they have colored the drawing? They are attention-seekers naturally and when they don't get that, "Wow, this looks amazing. Let's hang it on the fridge for daddy to see," they lose their confidence.

This takes us to the second important practice and that is, praising them when it's due. Holding back praise is another reason why some kids suffer from a lack of confidence in their lives. Positive feedback, even for adults, is an essential thing to have. So why deprive our kids of it? Praise them even if they have repeated the same practice for the hundredth time. Because what you don't know is that when they feel encouraged and praised, they try to do it better than the last time. Praises can also result in repeated actions, which is the perfect way to develop new habits such as persistence, resilience, and improved confidence.

Speaking of resilience, your child must also be taught that success isn't always a guarantee. This means there is a chance of setbacks and unexpected failures and pain. But they must know how to overcome and cope with such hardships without losing their confidence. Teaching resilience also means we promote the act of moving forward and not dwell on the failures for too long. More on this in Chapter 7, so stay tuned!

Next, you must, at all times and by all means, foster a growth mindset. Unlike a fixed mindset that suggests that humans are born with all the talents and skills they will ever possess, a growth mindset strongly believes in the possibility of learning new skills and cultivating talents over time. This is the kind of mindset you need your child to have.

Another way to build confidence is to help them in pursuing their passions. It is a no-secret secret that everyone acts more driven and passionate when it comes to doing something they love or are a fan of. Say, your child loves to draw. If you encourage them to follow their passion, take up additional advanced courses to improve their skills, they will feel more confident.

And finally, while helping them build confidence, don't forget to set goals that are achievable and tell them what is expected of them. Set uncomplicated rules that they can follow easily and don't be too hard on them when they fail to follow them. The goal shouldn't be to enforce rules and be strict, but to help them work around any setbacks and offer more clarity. When they know what is expected of them and how to get there, they will feel more confident.

Chapter 5: Taming the Monster Under the Bed

Did you know, one in every eight kids is affected by some type of anxiety? Untreated anxiety can develop into disorders, is hard to treat, and often results in poor school performance, increased absences, and missing out of important social experiences. Some research studies also suggest that it can drive kids and teenagers towards substance abuse (Lander, Howsare, & Byrne, 2013).

Anxiety is sometimes a fairly normal reaction to a given situation. Despite being seen as something bad, it needs to be comprehended as something preventive if it happens. All kids, big or small, experience anxiety at some point in their lives. It can be on graduation day, during an exam, or just when asked to make an introduction to the class. It has many phases that come and go. Think of a phase as something temporary. This means that it isn't harmful. However, kids who experience anxiety also report the development of other emotions like fear, shyness, or nervousness–emotions that can hinder their overall quality of life.

Some Common Signs of Anxiety

So, what does anxiety look like and how can parents know if their kids are being anxious or just excited?

There are some common signs to look for. For instance, a kid who suffers from bouts of anxiety may often cling onto someone (in the case that they are little), act scared or upset, cry, miss school, and be silent. They may also show a resistance when told to do something or do it wrong because their mind isn't where it should be. It is off somewhere wandering about the stress they are subconsciously experiencing. Some easy to notice symptoms include sweating, a worried look on their face, or nervousness that leads to shivering, shaking, or a racing heart.

When it starts to affect the body, that is when you really need to start worrying because anxiety can trigger a panic attack, which can make it harder for them to breathe. They may also complain of stomach aches or a dry mouth.

These symptoms that we associate with an anxious mind trigger the flight or fight response in the body. This is a normal response to an external threat or danger and humans have been experiencing it for ages. Anxiety releases chemicals in the brain that affect our nervous and digestive systems–preparing them to suit up for a fight. However, when anxiety attacks, this fight or flight response becomes overactive. So even when there is no danger present, the body tricks the mind into thinking there is and that is when all hell breaks loose.

Can Anxiety Be a Good Thing?

All that we have told you up to now about anxiety might have caused you to believe that it is a very bad thing. It is, most of the time. But there are times when this very emotion is the one that leads to greatness. Before we prepare parents to treat the symptoms of anxiety in their kids, how about we take a look at the claim we just made above.

Could anxiety be good?

Scientists believe that some extent of it is (Parker & Ragsdale, 2015). Referred to as eustress, good stress can serve as a motivating factor. There are some silver linings to it too and before wasting any more time, let's learn what they could be.

Anxiety can signal a warning. For instance, it can tell a child playing baseball, when to hit the ball or how to read the mind of the pitcher to anticipate the kind of swing they need to take. It brings awareness to the present and somehow slows down our minds to take in more information. Think of it as a slow-motion shot in a movie. Recurring worry and anxiety are signs that things need to change in your life and that your current state doesn't make you happy. When this happens, the child starts to explore ways and strategies to cope with it.

It can also serve as motivation as stated above. For instance, a child preparing for an exam the night before it is happening. Some level of anxiety about their exam will keep them focused on the revisions and enhance cognitive performance.

Anxiety also prepares us to battle a threat. Our bodies are wired to protect ourselves from danger and survive against all odds. When kids are faced with a challenge or tough situation and the anxiety creeps in, it can help them become more agile, process more information and radiate more energy. Notice how right after an accident, some bystanders can lift a full-size car and save the victim's life? That is anxiety doing its thing

What Can I Do to Help My Child?

Sometimes, when kids suffer from chronic anxiety that keeps them stuck under the covers out of fear, it can be hard for parents to cope. No one wants to see their kids suffer, especially from something they seemingly can't do anything about. In an effort to help them cope, they end up exacerbating it further. This is most common when parents try to take control and protect them from anticipated anxiety. But it isn't always the right thing to do. The goal should be to teach them how to cope with it on their own so that the next time they face it, they know what to do about it.

To help you get started, here are a few things you can do to calm them down.

Reassure Them

Worry is inevitable. If you know your child is worrying, no point in telling them not to worry. It seems like the right thing to do but what you have to do instead is, reassure them. Try to rationalize the worry using the FEEL method. The benefit of the feel method is that when kids are feeling stressed, their brain releases a dump of chemicals that makes them turn deaf to all the advice being given. It's not like they don't want to hear or listen to you, it's just that their brain doesn't allow them to. The prefrontal cortex, regulating logic and rationale goes numb and thus, they are unable to think clearly. This is where the FEEL method comes in. It stands for:

F: Freeze: The first thing you need to do is to tell them to pause and take deep breaths.

E: Empathize: Tell them that you understand what they are going through without offering any advice or suggestion. Just let them know that you get it.

E: Evaluate: This includes the task of problem-solving with them to find solutions to the problems. This comes after they are done being anxious and are all calmed down.

L: Let Go: This last one is for you, parents. In case you aren't successful in helping your child cope, don't let the guilt consume you. Let go of the notion that you are a bad parent.

Build a Relaxation Kit With Them

The best way to de-stress is to distract the young one with something else. For you, it might mean going for a walk or taking a bubble bath. For your kids, it can mean doing something they like doing. For example, if they love to color, you can create a kit including some drawing books and color boxes. If they are a fan of playing with action figures, you can have a bag full of them hanging behind their room's door.

These are meant to be relaxation kits, involving things they enjoy doing or are interested in. This will divert their mind and reduce the amount of anxiety they feel.

Talk It Out

If they are old enough to understand the emotion they are going through, there is nothing better than to have a talk with them about it like adults. They should know what is happening to their body and why. When kids don't understand that what they are going through is anxiety, it can be frightening. On the other hand, when they know what they have to deal with, they feel much more prepared and confident. Sit them down and help them recognize the feelings and triggers that induce anxiety. Reassure them that this will pass.

DIY a Worry Box

It doesn't have to be a box; it can also be a jar. The idea is to give them an activity that helps them recognize, analyze, and cope with what they are feeling. The trick is to write down the cause of the worry on a piece of paper and put it in the worry box. Tell them to take out the paper a week later and see if the worry is still there or worth causing anxiety. If it isn't, they can simply tear up the paper and feel freed from it.

Respect Their Feelings

If a child seems stressed about some upcoming event, respect their feelings but don't empower them. They should learn to deal with the event and be more prepared to face it. Validation is one thing and agreeing with them is another. So simply acknowledge but don't offer solutions. Let them come up with some on their own.

Chapter 6: Call Upon the Stage—Willpower

As kids grow, they face new challenges every day. In this fast-paced and competitive world, they have to rise above others to find their place in the world. When they feel confident enough to head for achievement, they need persistence and perseverance. These two require a ton of self-discipline and willpower.

Willpower or self-discipline refers to the ability to delay or avoid unhealthy excess of things. We have been told repeatedly throughout our lives that excess of anything is bad. One of the biggest advantages of self-discipline in the life of a child is that it allows them to willingly give up on the easy way of doing things and focus on doing them right. This eliminates shortcuts and instant gratification, which many opt for. However, self-disciplined kids know that the harder they work, the greater will be the reward. So they stay put, focus on the task at hand and don't give in to distractions—positive or negative.

We can understand self-discipline and willpower in several ways. The definitions of both are synonymously used to determine:

- The ability to not give up
- Perseverance
- Self-control

- Staying focused on the goals despite setbacks and failures

What Disciplining a Child Means

Discipline means teaching a child about guidelines, expectations, and principles. Children need to be regularly taught how to differentiate between what is good and bad for them. There are many ways to teach discipline. Some ways focus on increasing positive behaviors or decreasing undesirable ones. Others include the concept of rewards and punishments. Whichever method is used, the goal remains the same. It is to foster sound judgment in children so that they feel more confident to navigate their paths in life. Disciplining a child means that they learn to control their desires, negative emotions and feelings and learn to be responsible for their actions. It also means that they know that their actions will have consequences, so they need to be extra cautious about the choices they make. It also aims to teach them to own up to their mistakes but not hold onto them for the rest of their lives or quit because of them.

But how can it help beat negative behavior? How can we be sure that teaching them about having strong willpower will save them from any negative thoughts or at least, allow them to escape from them?

Beating Negativity With Self-Control

To beat negativity, your child just needs one thing–the right mindset or attitude. Attitude refers to the way we dedicated ourselves to how we think. If we think negatively, we will have a negative outlook on everything. If we think positively, we will notice the beauty in everything, even the things that are flawed. It's like your child's bicycle with pedals and brakes. If they want to stop, they can stop. If they want to keep going, they can keep going. It all comes down to their choice and self-control.

Below are some ideal tips and practices to start with your kid/kids so that they maintain a positive outlook or to put it more accurately–nip negativity before it starts to branch out and corrupt their little minds.

Teach them to be open and accept their mistakes. They need to come clean about when they make an oopsie and own it. Blaming others won't get them far, it will only make them feel like a victim. The first step they will take is to take responsibility for their actions and then for their emotions.

Secondly, let them know that they always have a choice. They can either call it quits or keep moving ahead. It is up to them. When discussing this, focus heavily on the positive aspects of moving forward and the drawbacks of giving up.

Teach them to look at mistakes and failures as lessons and not as roadblocks. If you want to beat negativity with strong willpower, then they must know that it is their thoughts that direct their actions. If they view their failures as a means of learning, they will know what mistakes to avoid making in the future. If they view them as crappy and stupid, they will choose to quit.

Give them examples of people they can look up to. Give them resources to learn about aspiring people. When they learn about the hardships these people had to go through and how, despite those difficulties, they made a name for themselves, it will motivate them to do the same.

Tell them to have an empathetic approach. The more giving and caring they are, the more they will be rewarded. Have you ever noticed how good things keep happening to good people? It is their thinking and humble approach towards others that win them a place in the world and in the hearts of others.

Help them come up with solutions, distractions, and ways to shift their gaze to the bright side of things. If they focus too much on what they don't have instead of what they do, they will always remain crybabies and worry too much. Teach them to see the glass as half-full and not half-empty.

And finally, let them know that complaining won't get them anywhere. If they aren't happy with something, they better create change. It is the only way to come out of a negative solution as a victor.

Chapter 7: Resilience to the Rescue

Imagine a world free from peer pressure, bullying, diseases, poverty, or death. Imagine if we had the power to save our kids from all such nuisances and cruel realities of life. Wouldn't that make it a much happier world to live in?

Since we unfortunately can't, we have to ensure that if the time comes, they are ready to take care of themselves, their feelings, and emotions. As parents, we want to protect them from everything that is bad, but for how long? How can we do that when they fly away from the nest and start their own families, careers, and separate lives? Our worries would still be the same. One of the biggest things anyone fears is change. And kids, well, they don't do well with it either. But change is inevitable. This means we have to work harder to prepare them for the unknown and life's uncertainties. We have to prepare them to not only face hardships and challenges and come out as victors but also to accept their failures and move on.

A resilient child is someone who knows how to bounce back from loss, grief, or failure. For them, it isn't just about surviving but rather viewing the negative outcomes and finding something positive in them. It is the uniqueness of resilient kids that unlike others, they are able to thrive and grow–no matter how big the setbacks.

Building resilience in kids is important for a number of reasons. For starters, it allows them to develop habits and coping mechanisms that will come in handy whenever they are faced with a challenging task or unexpected loss. It will prevent them from becoming overwhelmed by their emotions and let them determine the next course of action. Any step not taken with the right mind can have bitter consequences. Therefore, resilience helps kids find that balance in between their emotions and actions and come out of stressful times tactfully.

Secondly, resilience also allows kids to make healthy and calculated risks. They can do so because failure no longer seems like a threat. They don't fear the unexpected and are accepting of their mistakes when they make them. They also feel more confident to move beyond their comfort zones and explore daring options. In general, they are brave, curious and trust their instincts. All of these qualities aid them in achieving their goals and following their passions.

Resilient kids also face fewer mental health issues later in life. Although there is only some emerging evidence to imply a link, we still believe it possible. First, kids with mental health issues, such as chronic anxiety or depression have a negative outlook on life. They hold onto their past, mistakes, and failures. A lack of resilience renders them helpless to overcome them. So we can sense a pattern there.

How Resilience Beats Anxiety and Negativity

But the real question is this: can it beat anxiety and negativity? If you are looking for a one-word answer, then yes. Strong resilience and toughness can help get rid of negative thoughts. There are a few ideas worth sharing to help parents teach their children. These are aimed to help their children beat the crippling effects of anxiety and negativity on their mind and body.

Offer Them a Healthy Environment

As their parent, your foremost duty is to give them a healthy environment to survive in. They should engage in activities that help them stay calm and relaxed. They should be able to express themselves and be heard. They should be able to spend quality time with their parents and siblings fostering care, compassion, and affection. They should always feel supported and looked after.

Focus on Their Well-Being

Any child, who feels cared for and loved will be optimistic. Being loved by others offers us a sense of comfort. Your goal here should be to build a strong emotional connection with them. This requires that you help them problem-solve, listen to their worries and concerns, and show empathy. When children feel loved, they feel empowered to take chances. They know that they have a strong support system backing them and thus, they feel more confident to approach new things. It also builds their coping skills with negative emotions like anger, frustration, angst, or sadness.

Offer Opportunities to Take Healthy Risks

Parents should also offer their children a chance to step out of their comfort zones and indulge in something that challenges them. In a world when we have made playgrounds safe by installing bouncy floors, it is very hard to find ways to encourage them to take healthy risks. Healthy risk is something that doesn't involve too much danger but still allows the child with an opportunity to grow and learn. For instance, encouraging them to ride their bike without training wheels could be a start. This builds resilience in them over time, especially when they succeed.

Reframe Bad Experiences

Help kids see bad experiences in a more positive light. Ask them what they learned from those events and what changes they are planning to make to counter any mistakes the next time. Healthy discussions as such, open room for a new and improved perspective. Motivate them to look for the silver lining in all things—even failures and heartbreaks. If your teenage son just had a tough breakup, ask him to look at the reasons why it wasn't perfect in the first place and remind him not to repeat the errors the next time. Not only will it help with healing, but it will also build resilience.

Teach Them the Art of Letting Go

Lastly, to beat negativity, children have to learn to let go of the things in the past and focus on their present and future. The best way to outdo negativity is to give today a chance to be better. Teach them to acknowledge, accept, and let go of what happened in the past and move on. When they start to focus on their today and tomorrow, they will experience reduced stress and more anticipation for a happy future.

Chapter 8: Is My Child Emotionally Ready?

It is every parent's ultimate goal to raise an emotionally intelligent child. Emotional-intelligence, unlike general IQ, doesn't get enough limelight. However, it is starting to. This final chapter aims to give parents an overall idea about what emotional intelligence is, why their kids need it and how it can help break the cycle of negativity.

You must have noticed that nearly all the chapters before this have dealt with issues of either negative attitudes or anxiety. But we are yet to discuss what happens when negativity wins, when anxiety and stress get the best of our kids, and when the day seems less happy as we see our kids defeated by the hand of their inner critic. Who is responsible for what comes next? Why doesn't no one talk about the damage that happens afterward?

The foremost reason to raise emotionally-intelligent kids is so that they can manage the many emotions they experience and learn to regulate them on their own. Being emotionally intelligent allows kids to prevent a meltdown or temper tantrum before it happens and cope with their failures, loss, or grief in a more dignified and productive manner.

Understanding Emotional Intelligence

Emotional intelligence is an individual's ability to express, control, handle, and be conscious of the emotions they feel. It entails the art of being considerate towards ourselves and others and speak our minds better. On the whole, these are the things that an emotionally-intelligent child will portray. They can:

- Recognize and analyze the emotions of others and themselves.

- Possess emotional consciousness.

- Label their emotions and know how to express them.

- Understand how feelings and emotions affect mood, physical health, voice, body language, and state of mind.

- Build emotional vocabulary to better name the emotion they are experiencing.

- Bridge the gap between actions and emotions and how the latter can affect the former.

- Show sympathy towards others and be empathetic towards them.

Statistics reveal that nearly 10% of kids across the globe suffer from depression. This is alarming as we still don't have a cure for chronic depression. The kids who are depressed fail to deal with the emotions they feel, and thus, have an overall negative thought process. When one is depressed, the creative and rational parts of the brain become suppressed. This renders us hopeless when it comes to coping with what we feel and helpless in looking for a solution to counter it. Therefore, it is becoming highly crucial in today's age that we teach our children how to develop emotional intelligence and use it as a tool to combat negativity.

How a Mentally-Tough Mind Makes Combating Negativity Easier

Kids experience a wide range of emotions. These include both the positive and the negative. Usually, positive emotions are rewarded with praise, appreciation, and satisfaction. It is the other set of emotions that pose the real threat. Kids experience negative emotions too. Perhaps, someone from their class, other than them, got selected as the teacher's helper. Perhaps, someone well-deserving got kicked off the football team. Perhaps, they found out that their best friend wasn't a friend at all. It is okay to feel a range of negative emotions in these instances. There are endless scenarios we can list that breed negative emotions.

So how do we, as their parents, help them cope with those emotions better? How, using emotional intelligence, we can teach them to work through them without taking any drastic actions?

Is It Really Worth It?

Ask them if the problems they are facing now will be worth crying over in the future? Will an insignificant failure, like failing a class test, matter when they are older? Kids need to know to regulate their emotions from an early age. They must be made to understand which things are worth the effort and which aren't. If they experience a setback, ask them if it somehow hinders their long-term goals or not. Ask them, is it worth crying their out eyes over it? Ask them if it is worth the fight or would you be better off using your energy on something worthy? Knowing how the emotions they feel today determine their actions and possible outcomes in the future can help them make better choices.

Label the Feelings

When kids know what they are feeling, they can better feel the power they have over them. They need to be able to distinguish between anger and frustration, sadness and grief, worry and anxiety. When they know what they are dealing with, they cope with it better.

What Is the Other Person Thinking?

If the negative emotion involves someone other than your child, tell them to try wearing the other person's shoes for a moment and look at the situation from their perspective. For instance, if your child felt hurt because their friend didn't let them ride their new bike, ask them would they have done the same? Would they have allowed someone else to ride it, considering how choosy they are?

Viewing things from someone else's perspectives breeds a sense of empathy–an integral part of emotional intelligence. Your child will get an insider's look at how it feels like to be on the other end of the spectrum for once and build empathy and concern. They will also be less judgmental about things and try to view them from various mindsets too.

Prevents Immature Reactions

When kids know what they are feeling and why they are feeling it, it prevents them from reacting immediately or too hastily. When they are taught that reacting to a negative emotion never results in a positive outcome, they avoid reacting to them with an outburst. Instead, they look for means to cope with them and healthily distance themselves from them.

Conclusion

Throughout the book, we have labeled negative thoughts as bad or unwanted. However, did you know that if we never experienced them, we wouldn't have been able to make the distinction between which are good and which are bad for us? Keeping that in mind, it doesn't mean that we let our children experience negativity all the time. We need to teach them to manage it and keep it at bay. If we don't, it will wash away all their happy memories and opportunities of growth.

In this book, not only did we look at how to beat negative thoughts, but we also briefly discussed negativity's many friends that tag along with it. These include anxiety, stress, lack of self-confidence, poor resilience, and low self-esteem. All these emotions and disorders are the offspring of negative thinking. Therefore, to get rid of a negative mind and approach, we needed to tackle these first. And we did, hopefully!

We listed such means and strategies that will make parenting seem slightly less taxing and help parents raise optimistic and self-reliant kids. We also provided strategies and ways to nurture self-confidence in children so that they can prepare themselves for the world. There is not a doubt in our minds that by adopting these practices, our kids will learn to become resilient in the face of adversity and uncertainty and cope with negative emotions intelligently and empathetically.

Now that we feel more empowered, it is time we let the world know that we are ready to send our little soldiers out the door, sit back, and watch them succeed.

References

10 Tips for Parenting Anxious Children. (2016, February 29). Retrieved from https://www.webmd.com/parenting/features/10-tips-parenting-anxious-children

Deutschendorf, H. (2019, November 12). 5 Ways Emotional Intelligence Helps Us Manage Negative Emotions. Retrieved from https://thriveglobal.com/stories/5-ways-emotional-intelligence-helps-us-manage-negative-emotions/

Jain, R. (2017, September 7). 9 Things Every Parent with an Anxious Child Should Try. Retrieved from https://www.huffpost.com/entry/9-things-every-parent-with-an-anxious-child-should-try_b_5651006

Kanter, R. M. (2019, November 6). Overcome the Eight Barriers to Confidence. Retrieved from https://hbr.org/2014/01/overcome-the-eight-barriers-to-confidence

Kinderman, P., Schwannauer, M., Pontin, E., & Tai, S. (2013). Psychological Processes Mediate the Impact of Familial Risk, Social Circumstances and Life Events on Mental Health. PLoS ONE.

Lander, L., Howsare, J., & Byrne, M. (2013). The Impact of Substance Use Disorders on Families and Children: From Theory to Practice. Social work in public health, 194–205.

O'Shea, E. (2020, March 20). 6 Tips to Help your Negative Child. Retrieved from https://www.parent4success.com/2014/03/19/6-tips-to-help-your-negative-child/

Parker, K. N., & Ragsdale, J. M. (2015). Effects of Distress and Eustress on Changes in Fatigue from Waking to Working. Applied Psychology: Health and Well-Being, 293-315.

Schimelpfening, N. (2020, March 21). Symptoms of Clinical Depression. Retrieved from Verywell Mind: https://www.verywellmind.com/top-depression-symptoms-1066910

Star, K. (2019, September 29). Are There Potential Benefits to Having Anxiety? Retrieved from https://www.verywellmind.com/benefits-of-anxiety-2584134#citation-1

Tod, D., Hardy, J., & Oliver, E. J. (2011). Effects of Self-Talk: A Systematic Review. Journal of Sport and Exercise Psychology, 666-87.

HOW PARENTS CAN DEVELOP HAPPY CHILDREN

Uplifting Ways to Build Your Kids Social Skills to Transform Them Into Thriving and Successful Adults

Frank Dixon

© Copyright 2020 - All rights reserved.

The content contained within this book may not be reproduced, duplicated or transmitted without direct written permission from the author or the publisher.

Under no circumstances will any blame or legal responsibility be held against the publisher, or author, for any damages, reparation, or monetary loss due to the information contained within this book, either directly or indirectly.

Legal Notice:

This book is copyright protected. It is only for personal use. You cannot amend, distribute, sell, use, quote or paraphrase any part, or the content within this book, without the consent of the author or publisher.

Disclaimer Notice:

Please note the information contained within this document is for educational and entertainment purposes only. All effort has been executed to present accurate, up to date, reliable, complete information. No warranties of any kind are declared or implied. Readers acknowledge that the author is not engaged in the rendering of legal, financial, medical or professional advice. The content within this book has been derived from various sources. Please consult a licensed professional before attempting any techniques outlined in this book.

By reading this document, the reader agrees that under no circumstances is the author responsible for any losses, direct or indirect, that are incurred as a result of the use of the information contained within this document, including, but not limited to, errors, omissions, or inaccuracies.

Introduction

There's nothing more contagious than the laughter of young children; it doesn't even have to matter what they're laughing about. — **Criss Jami**

Happy kids, ah, don't we all want them?

Those uncontrollable laughs, those smiley faces, gleaming eyes and pouts and kisses on our cheeks... there isn't anything more joyful than to parent a child.

Whenever any parent, like yourself, is asked that crucial yet thought-provoking question, "What do we want most for our kids?" We often face a dilemma between happiness and success. Success does matter, but it would mean nothing without happiness and satisfaction. We can do without success but seeing our kids unhappy is just heartbreaking. We want them to have the best experiences possible, protect them from heartaches and pull them up in our arms whenever they fall. This is just who we signed up to be.

But there is one thing that we fail to realize. While we want them happy and cheerful, we end up doing more wrong than right. Remember *Charlie and the Chocolate Factory*? Remember Veruca Salt and how her father just wanted her to have everything to keep her happy? Well, that didn't turn out good for her, did it?

Trying to make our kids happy had been once considered the key to success but not anymore. Today, it is viewed as a negative influence and known to be raising unhappy and fragile young adults. While we think that bowing to all their requests would make them happy, we fail to see that it also promotes dependency and escalates negativity. They start to throw temper tantrums when they are refused and resort to the display of negative emotions.

Maybe they are crying for a new toy today. Maybe they just want to stay up past midnight once or eat ice-cream when down with the flu. When children are served their preferences quickly, it makes them dependent. They may be happy for a while, but it won't last long.

But how dare we? How dare we tell parents to do the opposite? It's outrageous and beyond belief. You may feel like giving up on the book entirely but hear us out.

Our goal, as parents, isn't to make them happy but to teach them how to be. This is the difference we are aiming to address here.

When we use the former approach and presume that it is our job to make them happy, we are raising them to rely on someone else for their happiness. Might seem like a small thing but the more you let that thought sink in, the better.

Your job shouldn't be to make them happy but to raise them as adults who don't rely on others to feel a certain way. If this continues, they will always be looking at others to make them feel complete and wholesome and become prone to heartbreaks. It's a lot like telling them to jump from a plane without a parachute and hoping that someone will catch them before they fall to their deaths. We know it is a harsh example to put but you need to get to the depth of it.

We worry and want you to worry too!

Don't set them up for failure or sign up to be their emotion coach. Let them be their teacher. If there is something that needs teaching, let it be social skills. Teach them to master a new skill, teach them to learn a new language, teach them to be empathetic, teach them to be kind, teach them to be considerate of others and most importantly, teach them to regulate their emotions.

Developing their social skills is the greatest gift to give to a child. Helping them navigate their path to success, follow their passion, be empathetic and self-reliant are the skills that will help them make a name for themselves in the world.

According to one study conducted by the researchers at Pennsylvania State and Duke University, prosocial behavior is a predictor of success (Jones, Greenburg, & Crowley, 2015). The study tracked some 700 children for twenty years, from their childhood to them becoming young adults and concluded that kids who develop social skills early in their childhood seemed to have more promising careers and well-being. Children that lacked basic social skills like anger management, emotional regulation, independence, discipline, and good communication skills displayed a higher dependency and inclination towards drug and substance abuse later in life. The researchers also predicted that they also had a higher chance of being involved in criminal activities and spending jail time.

Keeping that in mind, this book aims to help parents develop social skills in their children from an early age to improve their chances of being happy and successful in their future. It is high time we start focusing on the things and habits that will help them prosper and thrive for success rather than giving in to their demands and setting them up for instability in their emotions and reduced chances of success in the future.

Chapter 1: Social Skills – What Are They?

Children enter this world relying on others. For the first few months, they rely completely on others for feeding and changing. As their senses begin to sharpen, they start to make sense of the world around them, get accustomed to the familiar faces around and begin to form a bond. They become picky like preferring to be in the arms of a sibling or relative instead of a stranger, feel anxiety, fear, and stress when separated for long. It is the time when they start to have social interactions with the people around them.

The next couple of years, referred to as the toddlerhood, and are more about knowing themselves. They start to desire and demand things, notice and imitate actions and behaviors and explore the world around, once again by relying on their five senses. As they start kindergarten, they are presented with many opportunities to develop social skills. For instance, they learn to share things with others, form proper sentences to communicate better and learn to label the many emotions they go through. If all goes well and they pick up fairly well, they continue to grow – both cognitively and socially.

Social skills allow us to deal with others in a sophisticated and healthy manner. It is what keeps interactions positive and nurturing. Children with effective social skills, be it in the communication, listening or anger management area, can express themselves more clearly, respectfully and in a calm manner. They are empathetic and show concern and worry about the feelings of others. They know when to listen and behave. They know how to regulate their emotions. They own up to their mistakes and don't blame others for their shortcomings and wrong estimations.

Our kids learn social skills via experiences and interactions they have with the people around them. These include their parents, peers, friends, and relatives. The development of social skills is essential for several reasons. For example, they help kids prosper and thrive for a successful, more fulfilling life on their futures. It also helps them create a roadmap of how they wish to follow their heart and give their passions the ignition they need to become a reality. They also teach kids how to avoid negative emotions or at least, prevent themselves from overreacting to them or letting them overpower them and alter their behavior from positive to negative. Social skills give them opportunities to grow and have meaningful relationships too. Not to forget, the good our children are at exhibiting social skills, the more confident they will be and exercise more control of their lives.

The development of social skills also prepares them for a self-reliant life. After all, we can't always be ahead of them, navigating their path for them and saving them from falling in dark and hidden pit holes. They have to take the reins in their hands someday. So why not set them on the right path from today? Why not give them what they need so that they no longer have to rely on others for it?

It seems rather wise and logical, doesn't it? Think about it, when they display good manners, are good at taking instructions and following suit, they become more aware of themselves and their surroundings. They learn how to deal with different people in different ways. It is their key to opening the gateway of enhanced experiences and increases their chances of success and happiness. When they feel more in control of their life and feel all-set to steer their way forward, we become the ones to cheer for them in the stands. We don't hold their hand or drag them through the race of life –they learn to do it themselves. Nothing more can offer the sense of pride all parents secretly crave. They want their kids to talk of the town and be recognized for all the good in their hearts, the decency in their manners and the excellence in their upbringing.

Kids, like most adults, are socially-adept. They know how to make friends and show empathy towards others when they sense sadness, anxiety or hurt. Even if they aren't too friendly and don't engage with people too often, there is little to worry about, because social skills can be learned and nurtured with time. In this book, you will come across many such exercises, activities, and games to enhance their social skills and develop them into happy kids. They are super-easy, to begin with, and work well for kids of all ages.

Essential Social Skills in Children

No point in discussing the Kardashians or the Hiltons as our children become the ultimate socialites when they have developed good social skills. From the minute they had been born, they had been expanding their social interactions with every gaze, stare, and expressions. They had conversations with their parents and siblings long before they were able to speak full sentences. They have shown anger when deprived of some need, they have caused a fuss when told 'no,' and they have smiled and laughed when we made stupid faces at them and whatnot. The point is, they have been showing us that they already are born with nearly all the social skills they would ever need, they just need you to help them understand and enhance them. For instance, if they are frustrated, they want you to make them feel better if they are sad, they want you to make them feel happy and alive again. They know what to do, they just need some tips to be good at them.

So, before we head onto the next chapter and talk about the relationship between happiness and social skills in detail, let's do a quick overview of the essential social skills your child needs help with.

1. Communication: Effective communication is as essential for kids as it is for adults. Children, from a young age, should be taught to express themselves comfortably and be good listeners. They must know how to

apologize to someone when they have wronged them and listen when schooled over a certain behavior.

2. Interpersonal Skills: These skills involve the art of sharing, seeking permission and joining activities. It is about building healthy relationships with everyone without feeling envious, jealous or bitter.

3. Empathy: Empathy is a chance to hear and understand others. It entails being in someone else's shoes and viewing things from their perspective for a change. It is about identification with the feelings of others and young children must know that too.

4. Conflict management: Kids must develop skills that prevent fights and make situations less threatening. They should be taught to reason with logic in a cool manner so that the other person doesn't take offense or engage in a fight. It includes getting to the source of the issue and finding means to work it out without losing patience.

5. Problem-solving Skills: Kids should be taught to look for solutions to their problems themselves. If required, they should also know how to seek help

without feeling ashamed or like a complete failure.

6. Patience: This is a hard one to teach as impatience is the other name of being a kid. They must know when to stay put and be quiet. They must know that others also need to be heard. They must learn to wait for their turn and know how to share.

7. Direction: Another pivotal skill is to follow directions and stay away from things they are told to stay away from. Kids who lack these often report behavioral issues later in life and are always getting themselves in trouble.

8. Anger Management: Knowing the difference between reacting and responding is a crucial aspect of managing anger and frustration. This skill focuses on helping kids learn to express themselves in a calm and composed manner, despite feeling overpowered with negative emotions.

9. Acceptance of Differences: This is often one of the most underrated skills for kids of today to have. The lack of this skill is what develops bullies. Kids who don't know how to accept and appreciate differences often suffer when building

relationships. They feel privileged and disregard anyone that doesn't look like them. They need to be taught that everyone is unique in their way and therefore, respected equally.

Chapter 2: Social Skills and Happiness – Is There A Connection?

We have quoted the same several times in the book already but is it true? Does the development of social skills help kids prosper in life, lead them on the road to success and make them happy? These are all big arguments, debatable and great conversation starters for parents when together on a playdate or a soccer practice. Therefore, this chapter is aimed at offering some great points, all backed by research and scientific backing, some even following up for two decades. While stressing on finding that connection between social skills and happiness, we shall learn more about the importance of social skills development.

Social Interactions, Empathy, and Compassion

Developing positive social relationships, a type of social skills has also been linked with happiness, improved health and longevity. Good interpersonal relationships with the people around us not only adds more value to our personality, but it also helps us climb the stairs of success. The more people we know and are on good terms with, the more willing they are to help us reach our long-term goals. The more helpful and cooperative we are with others, the greater the chances of succeeding.

This is what likability does. In his book titled, *Give & Take*, Adam Grant, a Wharton professor suggests that when we hold compassion for others in our hearts and hope to build supportive relationships, instead of staying immersed in ourselves, we increase our chances of becoming someone in the future. We all know that good attracts good and this just proves that.

Another research points out that kids are intrinsically compassionate. They wear their heart on the sleeve and know how to love and share. However, as they grow older and get introduced to the various technological distractions that focus on them alone, they become self-absorbed and stop caring about others.

Ever wonder why our parents and grandparents had such a calm and loveable relationship? They seemed rather happy and content with the life they had. Psychologist Jean Twenge, in her book, *Generation Me* writes about the many changes in the lifestyles of our parents and our kids. According to her, we have bombarded our kids with screen time, social media and meaningless activities that add no value to their intellect and social skills. On one side, the media keeps fueling them with hatred, jealousy, and biases and on the other, social media platforms grab them by the collar and keep them engaged for hours at once. We have allowed them to become the generation that rarely looks up and sees the beauty of nature. We have made them self-absorbed and competitive kids for all the wrong reasons. They don't feel compassion towards others but they would enjoy looking at violence (video games).

But none of this promises content and happiness. It only gives heed to unwanted competition as to who follows the next trend in the coolest manner or takes the best selfie.

As their parents, we have to turn back the time and nurture compassion in them – something they were born with. We have to encourage them with the right tools and activities like volunteer work, taking them to the zoo to know about the animal kingdom and foster habits like empathy and kindness in them so that they learn to consider the needs of others too. That surely increases their chances of succeeding in life and experiencing the pure joy that comes from helping someone out.

Think about it, if we all worked together as a unit, there would be no competition to beat and no standards to live up to.

Social Skills and Relationships

Social skills also increase our chances of being liked. We love our kids dearly, but we also want them to be loved by others and experience what it's like to love unconditionally. As it turns out, sharp social skills are all that you need to do just that. When your child is socially-adept, they can express themselves in a convincing, articulate and alluring way. They can empathize with others, understand their grievances and motivation. They can feel comfortable expressing their thoughts and ideas with others more openly. They can learn to adapt and sacrifice their ego if it makes their friends or partners happy. They can decently manage their feelings and emotions.

Picture this: Your child is at a school play and ready to play their part on the stage. One of their classmates gets stage fright and their friends are of no help. Instead of boosting him to get over the fear, they all joke about it, make fun and wait for the poor soul to make a laughing stock of himself. Now, your child has two choices. Either they join the club of the laughing harassers or help the kid with stage fright get over his fear. If they are compassionate and empathetic, they will choose to side with the classmate. They will rush to offer help and moral support. One of the teachers witnesses it and at the end of the play makes all parents stand up and applaud to praise your child for standing up against bullies.

Now imagine the same scenario in an office with a new employee on his first day, a bunch of colleagues ready to roast him and your child is the only support the new employee has. The manager sees you comforting the new team member and appreciates your effort in front of everyone during the meeting.

Who, by the end of the day, gets the bigger reward? Your child who helped the new employee settle in or those other colleagues who did nothing but to upset him?

This suggests that connecting with people improves your likeability and leaves a positive impression on others. It also helps to nurture good relationships.

The point is this: despite showing your kid with all the jewels and gadgets in the world if they fail to connect with others and find like-minded people, they will be at a loss. All the money in the world will not be enough to make them experience true happiness and joy if they aren't able to connect with others.

Social Skills – A Predictor of Success?

If you assume that specialized technical skills are what helps people get ahead in the job market, you couldn't be more wrong. We are living in a world where something new replaces the old every passing day. Who would have thought a decade ago that we will no longer have to waste time watching ads on TV and enjoy Netflix, HBO or Disney+ ads-free at a minimum fee?

In a fast-paced economy, humans will soon be replaced by machines and AI and the only thing that will help us get ahead and still have a career and job is social skills.

According to one study, nearly half of the people in the United States will be jobless in the next 20 years as automation will take over (Manyika, et al., 2017). When asked what workers were supposed to do, David J. Deming suggested "becoming more human." Being a Harvard professor, Deming believes that social skills will be considered a valued asset and will become increasingly important. His findings suggest that the coming years will value cognitive and social skills more than jobs requiring high-levels of analytical or mathematical training but little social prowess. They will become obsolete and be taken over by machines and advanced technology.

So when jobs become automated, there will be fewer human resources required and only those will make the cut who are good at relationship management and client satisfaction. The value and growth rate for those able to exercise innate human qualities like empathy and kindness will increase, because this is, sadly the only thing that computers can't master. When teams will become exponentially smaller, it is these skill sets that will come in handy. Flexibility will be rewarded and so will social aptitude.

This means that by the time your children are in their 20s and 30s, it won't matter if they can memorize tables by heart or if they can solve complex math problems, what will matter is how socially-adept they are. How flexible, compassionate and benevolent they are. So why not work on that and stop worrying about getting a better tutor for them to ace in school.

Social Skills and Happiness

People who seem happy in general, have more people they hang out with. Their social circle seems bigger and they find it easy to become friends. However, social interactions go beyond just that. A question regarding social engagement and whether it has a link to our happiness and satisfaction was explored by Julia Rohrer, Martin Brummer, David Richter, Stefan Schmukle, and Gert Wagner in a 2008 paper. The question was simple: If you were more socially engaged the next year, would it make you happy?

The responses that were studied came from a large-scale survey conducted in Germany each year. Other questions accompanying the first one were also asked. They included questions about life satisfaction and strategies they would use to improve their satisfaction in the future.

The researchers focused on the collected data between 2014 and 2015. There were 1,500+ responses used as samples from participants that answered the questions both years. Out of those, 150 participants strongly believed that their lives won't change for the better in the future and thus their responses were omitted from the sample.

The remaining participants had listed strategies that would make them happier in the coming years. It was surprising to note that half of the respondents wrote about the "things" that might happen to them, which will make them happier. The other half wrote strategies that they would do to increase their happiness in the future.

The strategies were then reviewed and the researchers evaluated the ones that involved an increase in social engagement over time. Many respondents listed things like eating healthier, getting into good shape and finding a better job. However, these didn't qualify as they didn't have any aspect of social interactions. Some people wrote about spending more time with their friends or family or doing charity work and volunteering. These involved the element of an increase in social interactions.

The people that listed a social strategy, compared to those that wrote a non-social activity, showed equal happiness in the first year i.e. 2015. However, the happiness levels of those who wrote about a social strategy increased in the second year i.e. 2016. When compared with those who wrote a non-social strategy, they seemed happier and reported greater satisfaction.

But the researchers still needed to look at other aspects of what could have resulted in this type of difference in their happiness. So they got back to the samples to look for something else. As it turns out, those who had listed a social strategy have also listed an increase in the amount of time spent in social interactions. They deliberately wanted to spend more time with their loved ones and thus, their happiness was more evident.

The findings concluded that when we try to engage with people more explicitly, we tend to do things that make us socially-connected. When we feel supported, loved and cared for, it makes us happier.

The same is true for our kids. When they feel loved, have all their requests attended to and, heard, they feel satisfied and happy. However, all this isn't possible if they are not social or lack basic social skills like communication and listening and engagement. If we go back to the first line after the subtitle, it clearly states that socialites are happier. So the key DOES lie in developing the social skills needed to have a good life and experience true happiness.

Chapter 3: Listening and Communication

Some kids just don't know when to talk and when not to. Others don't know what to talk about or continue an ongoing conversation. Some struggle with initiation and only reply when spoken to. Some kids don't know how to listen and comprehend what is being said. The reason we want to focus on building effective communication and listening skills in kids is that we see it as the source of enhancing the others.

Ask yourself this: if my child lacks basic communication and listening skills, will they be able to have good conflict management, empathy, cooperating, and friends making skills?

How will they reach out to help others, talk to them, have their ideas heard if they don't know how to communicate well?

Picture this: You are at a family gathering with your child and everyone is having a good time eating dinner. The desserts are being served and everyone seems excited to try the rich chocolate delicacy that is the molten lava cake. One of your brother's fiancé is seated in front of your child. She happens to be a little on the heavier side. As she reaches for her plate of the desert, your child tells her that she shouldn't have cake as she is already so fat.

Wouldn't you just melt with shame and embarrassment? Wouldn't you want that the ground bursts open and engulfs you in it?

This happens when kids aren't taught basic conversation etiquettes from an early age or they have been encouraged too much to forget the distinction between right and wrong. What they need is a basic understanding of what is acceptable and what isn't and you have to be the ones to teach them that.

As both, communicating and listening hold critical importance, we are going to be looking at each individually and help readers understand their value and need.

How to Talk to Everyone

Social communication in children refers to how they use language within social surroundings and situations. When kids are young and naïve, they don't always know how to act in social gatherings and assume that they can be as carefree and careless as they are at home. This means that they can also behave in the same manner they behave at home with their siblings or parents. Social communication involves the learning of skills to engage in conversations. These include the words we use, how we say them, what our body language is when we say them and whether it is acceptable or not, given the situation. In the earlier example, the child lacked all of these skills. Communication skills are vital because they allow us to express ourselves and speak our minds. If we aren't able to do that, it can suppress them forever and leave behind a confused and caged mind. Good communication skills also allow us to access the situation first, address the cues and body language of the person we are conversing with and then form a sensible and situation-appropriate response.

In a nutshell, the development of effective communication skills in children from an early age helps them:

- Learn to express themselves clearly
- Convey and share their thoughts and ideas with others without feeling shy or unconfident
- Facilitate meaningful exchange with others that results in better relationships
- Boost your child's social IQ when they have more and more evocative interactions
- Help them do better academically because when kids are good at communicating verbally, they are also good at writing
- They have a reduced chance of developing mental health problems such as depression or social withdrawal

Activities That Encourage Communication

If you ask a kid, what is the best way to teach something to them, they will most probably come up with explanations like, via play, visuals or interaction? It is true, interactions, where the learner doesn't feel like they are being taught, is the most effective way to teach something new and important. There is less pressure that way for them to keep up and feel like they are being schooled. Hey, you can't blame the kids for thinking like that. We all wished that our studies were more interesting than just cramming answers from notes or a book. As the advancement of visual aid allows more visual interactions, the process of teaching has changed drastically. Therefore, to help all parents struggling with either a shy, naughty, hyperactive or self-absorbed kid lacking basic communication skills, here are three starter activities to try with them to teach them about how to be more expressive and communicative.

Turn-Taking

Teach them to take turns while conversing. The best way to do so is to have them seated beside you and pick a theme to talk about. You can even prepare notes to choose from and place them in a jar. Ask your child to pick and unfold and then ask them to talk about it for 1 minute straight.

Or you can simply write different colors on the notes, make them pick one and then list all the items they see of that color in the room they are in. You can give them 10 seconds to list the items and then, you pick a note and repeat the same. The idea is to teach them the importance of waiting for their turn to talk.

Show and Tell

This next one is quite similar to the first one. This involves a theme which the child, parents, and siblings discuss. For example, you can ask them about their favorite color, favorite shoes, favorite movie, or favorite book. Then when they list their favorite, you ask them why they chose it. They have to come up with at least five reasons why they chose it. For example, if they picked apple as their favorite fruit, their reasons could be:

- It is tasty
- It is red and I like the color red
- It is juicy
- It is very sweet and chewy
- It is easy to draw on a paper

This activity not only encourages communication but also builds their confidence.

Picture Storytelling

Picture storytelling is another great idea for a game. There are multiple directions you can take it in. For starters, you can share with them a picture and ask them to come up with a story about what they think is happening in it. Or you could offer them a set of pictures and ask them to arrange them in order. Or you could again provide them with a single picture and ask them to come up with descriptions for the characters in it. You can find a ton of pictures online. Have them printed and get busy playing.

Additional Tips and Info

Below are some additional tips for partners to teach their kids about the importance of good communication skills and how to help them improve over time.

- Make communication an essential part of your daily routine. This means you talk as much as you can with your child and encourage them to get involved too. Even if they are bad at staying engaged or have trouble starting conversations, be their guide and help with responding to you.

- When driving with them someplace, talk about the many things you two see throughout the ride. Engage them with interesting questions like, "If you could go anywhere right now, where would it be?" or "Do you see that blue car on the road? Let's see how many more blue cars we can spot before we drop you off to school." You may notice that both questions entice excitement and interest. They provoke the little one to think about their answer, pay attention to the road and have their mind open to possibilities.

- Be open and encouraging to talk about feelings, especially the negative ones so that you can help them develop an emotional vocabulary. Whilst at it, help them come up with solutions to those problems so that, whenever shortly, they experience that, they know what to do.

- Seek their opinion about things. For instance, ask them what they would like to do on their free day or what they would like to have for dinner. These may seem unimportant to you, but being validated and involved is a big thing for your kid. When they feel that their say means something and holds value, they become more expressive about them.

- And finally, make it a habit to read to/with them every night. The sooner they grasp new words, the more elaborate their vocabulary will be. The more elaborative their vocabulary, the more expressive they will be.

- Read together. Encourage them to read aloud to you and help them read a difficult word when they come across one. This will also build their confidence in themselves.

How to Listen Attentively

Listening doesn't mean you stay quiet and let the other speak. It means taking what is being told, comprehending it and then forming a decent reply when asked. With children suffering at the hands of poor attention span, it is one of the most critical social skills to develop early on. They must pay heed to what is being told no matter what they are engaged in. This requires not just a strong between the speaker and the listener but also good manners. The art of listening has some rules they must be taught to abide by. As parents, it is on us if they choose to misbehave in public or ignore something casually.

Besides, listening is something they had been doing for long – even when they were in the womb. The parents' voice was the only form of connection they had. So if it is something that they have the natural tendency for, why is it so hard for them to not do it naturally later on?

There are several reasons for this and one of them is the lack of basic social skills. They don't listen to you because they haven't been told to. Despite the reasons, you can't argue with the fact that the benefits of good listening skills are worth teaching. For example:

- It improves their communication and broadens their vocabulary.
- When they listen, it adds to their existing knowledge
- It makes following instructions and orders easier
- It develops their comprehension and literacy
- When kids listen, they pick up on advice and suggestions better
- It aids in their social development as most kids these days have a low attention span. Listening effectively is the opposite of that.

Fun Games to Improve Listening Skills

And again, we are back with some interesting and engaging activities and games to foster effective listening in kids. These are games we have played too when we were young and their simplicity is what makes them so unique and promising.

Simon Says

Haven't we all played it when we were younger too? Seems like it doesn't get old. The rules are simple: your child has to pay attention to what has been ordered or ordered not to do and follow the command. Whenever the command doesn't begin with Simon says, your child doesn't have to do it.

Therefore, there are two things that your child will have to be careful about:

1. Do they have to follow or not follow a certain order
2. What they must do once they have heard it

We Went to the Zoo and Saw a...

This is a more advanced game to play with older kids like adolescents or teenagers as it involves not just listening but also memorization. As the name hints, it starts with one partner, preferably you, saying the name of an animal that you saw at the zoo and then the other person, your child, repeating the same and adding another animal to it. Then when your turn comes again, you have to repeat the first two animals and add a third one to the list. Here's an example:

- We went to the zoo and saw a cheetah...
- We went to the zoo and saw a cheetah, a monkey...
- We went to the zoo and saw a cheetah, a monkey, and a giraffe...
- We went to the zoo and saw a cheetah, a monkey, a giraffe, a panda...

The animals must be listed in the said sequence and it is your child's job to remember them. Continue to play for as long as one of you makes a mistake and then you restart it. You will be amazed at how many animals can a child memorize.

Pick the Odd One Out

This is more like a test than a game but an interesting one. This demands complete attentiveness from your child. To begin, pick a category or theme. The rules are simple. They have to listen and pick out the odd word you said that doesn't belong to the chosen theme or category. For example, if you are listing animals and you say, rose somewhere in between, they have to stop you immediately. If they miss the odd word the first time, insert another odd thing and see if they can get it this time around.

You can start it with something simple as fruits, vegetables, pets or stationery items and then move onto more difficult categories that require more attentiveness.

Additional Tips and Info

Here is some more advice to follow the activities mentioned above.

- Let them finish first and then respond. This tells them about the importance of active listening and sets a good example for them to follow

- Use understandable words. Often when we use tough words in a sentence, the mind gets stuck on that sentence without the following suit to the rest of it. This leads to poor listening. Therefore, make it a habit to talk to a kid like a kid.

- When instructing or ordering them to do something, be very specific and clear about the expectations you have from them. Mixed messages are confusing for their developing brain.

- Don't use sarcasm, taunts or criticism. Be calm when explaining to them what behavior or action you don't want them to repeat when you are angry with them.

- When giving instructions, ask them to repeat back what has been said to check if you two are on the same paths

- Encourage reading out loud. To improve listening, take aid from audiobooks and always be eager to discuss any story they have just listened to.

Chapter 4: Empathy

As more and more venomous, deep-seated and disturbing news make the headlines, it is often hard to think of a life free of them. Was everything always this negative or has it become this vitriol recently? Whatever is the answer, we as parents, have to be more cautious than ever about the things we are exposing our kids too. Although it is good to have them stay updated about what's happening in the world, somewhere deep down, we also know that such violence, shown repeatedly, becomes a norm. Things like kindness, sympathy and understanding the emotions and feelings of others are no longer shown as strong qualities.

So, to develop a happy child in such chaos requires more practice than ever. When we were young, our parents never had to worry about such negative exposure. However, parents of today must – for the wellbeing of their kids and raise them to be above all this hate and bitterness.

This is where the act of empathy comes in.

Empathy is the ability to understand the feelings and emotions of others and put yourself in their shoes. It is about being kind and compassionate towards others and not being judgmental or sarcastic. It is one of the most important foundations of leading a happy life surrounded by loved ones. Think about it, who would want to be friends with someone egoist, racist or unkind? Someone who is always making fun of others and belittling them. Someone who thinks that the whole world revolves around them and doesn't respect the feelings of others? You wouldn't, right? Then, will you be okay if your child grows up to become one?

Studies suggest that empathy is a key factor in the building of healthy relationships. It helps grown-ups do well in work and find like-minded friends and partners. In a child's life, it means the formation of strong friendships that last a long time, good rapport with everyone and compassion for others.

However, did you know that kids are naturally egocentric? But hey, don't be quick to judge. We made them that way. Ever since they were born, we have been catering to nearly all of their demands and adjusting our lives according to their schedules. It is only fair that they feel a little privileged. Here's the good news: As empathy is a skill and not a talent, it is easy to instill along with other good habits like honesty, kindness, and discipline.

What Empathy Is?

In literal terms, empathy is a way humans connect with others. It is the art of developing an understanding of the way others feel and expressing compassion instead of judgment. It involves active listening and validation of the feelings of others. It also involves trying to look at the world from someone else's perspective and comprehending the reasons why they act the way they do/did.

But it isn't sympathy. Many confuse it to be but it isn't. When we are sympathetic, we feel sorry for them and while doing so, we unintentionally, look down on them instead of helping them or trying to understand what they are going through.

Why Care for Others

"But mom, why do I have to care about others?"

This is one of the many innocent questions your kid will ask when you teach them about the importance of being empathetic. This is the part where you have to talk with them about the many benefits it offers such as:

- Being empathetic allows them to develop stronger relationships with their friends and family.
- Being empathetic facilitates in building a sense of security
- Being empathetic helps build tolerance and acceptance
- Being empathetic promotes good wellbeing and mental health
- Being empathetic puts an end to the bullying culture in schools and workplaces
- Being empathic is how one can promote social harmony

- Being empathetic leads to lower levels of stress and negative emotions

- Being empathetic allows them to understand where others are coming from

- Being empathetic increases their chances of success in managerial positions when they grow older

Activities That Foster Empathy

Learning about empathy or any other good habit shouldn't feel like a chore to your kid. This is why, the best way to foster good habits and social skills like empathy, is through activities and games that they would enjoy. The moment we use the term 'activities,' many parents assume they would include some arts and crafts and cutting and drawing, but the ones mentioned below won't require much... Promise!

Take a look and get teaching.

Role Play

The biggest challenge when teaching kids about empathy is how to make them see what the other feels. How can they pretend to feel what someone is going through if they don't go through it themselves? This is where acting out scenarios comes into play (quite literally). Make a list of pretend scenarios and ask your child how they would feel if they were in that situation. Their answers will let you know how little/much work you need to do more to instill this habit for good. To get you started with some scenario examples, here are a few:

- Not getting invited to a birthday party
- Not getting good marks in a project they worked hard for
- Canceling of the trip they had been planning for, last minute
- Death of a pet suddenly
- Getting scolded wrongly by a parent etc.

Ask them to be as descriptive as possible when describing their reactions and feelings. Next, brief them about the importance of empathy.

Emotions Charades

Whenever we teach our kids about the importance of listening, communicating and empathy, we rarely put any emphasis on the non-verbal cues that are a form of communication too. Body language, poster, the look in someone's eyes, shivering in their hands and stutter in their voice are all signs that an empathetic listener can decipher. Therefore, this next exercise or activity is to teach them the power of empathy via non-verbal cues.

Get a few emoticons or emotions printed on a piece of paper. Cut each emotion into a small card. Ask your child to depict the expression they feel suits best with the emotion. For instance, if the card says happy, they might resort to smiling. As for the rules, you have to be completely unaware of what the card reads and place them in front of your forehead so that only they can read it – like traditional charades. This will improve their awareness about what different emotions look and feel like as they act them out themselves. So, the next time they see someone exhibiting one, they can understand better.

Temperature Check

This isn't an activity but rather an act of showing concern. You ask your child to have a seat beside you and ask them one simple question: "how are they feeling today?" You can have multiple members of the family playing the game so that everyone can have a say about how they are feeling. It is ideal to include some negative emotions too like sadness and anger so that later, you can have a discussion about it with your kid and tell them that it is completely normal to feel that way too.

Take a Quiz

Similar to the temperature check, this also involves some fun yet important questions to ask your child to understand them better. You write a few questions on a sheet of paper and then ask them to come up with an answer. The questions have to be these or something similar:

- How do we spot if someone isn't feeling good?

- How do we know when someone feels left out?

- How can we know what someone feels?

- What can we do to cheer up those who aren't feeling happy?

You can look up for more such questions online and let your child have a go at them. The goal is to understand how empathetic/ unsympathetic they are? When you know that, you will know how much effort you need to make to help them become empathetic.

Empathy Busters

Empathy busters, as the name suggests, is a fun activity that encourages children to understand what empathy busters are and how they can avoid them. For convenience, we have used the mnemonic SUDS to describe the four most common empathy busters. They are as follows:

1. S: Sarcasm – Saying things that are mean as a response to someone's unfortunate situation. For example: "Oh poor you, what a shame you fell in the puddle."

2. U: Unsolicited Advice – Some children try to offer suggestions and advice, thinking it will help the one in trouble. Sometimes, the one in trouble just wants to be understood and not told what to do next. So teach your kid not to present

their opinions about something unless asked for.

3. D: Dismiss Feelings – This refers to making one feel that the emotion they are feeling is wrong and shouldn't be felt. Saying things like, "You are just being dramatic," "it isn't a big deal, really…" feel wrong.

4. S: Solving the Issue – We all want to be heroes and saviors of the day. Sometimes, a person may only require to be heard. Trying to offer quick fixes is another no-no as the person may feel invalidated or dismissed.

Once your child is aware of these empathy busters, ask your child to recall a memory where they felt upset. Then ask them, what did others offer them? Did they show empathy or did they use one of the SUDS?

When they know what someone did and what they should have done, they will know how it feels and avoid putting someone else in that same situation again.

Additional Tips and Info

Want to develop a happy child who values the emotions and feelings of others? Here's how you can start:

- Empathize with them so that they follow suit. Kids see you as their role models and if you practice empathy with them, your partner, friends and family, they will learn to do the same.

- Teach them ways to show empathy towards others. They should know of ways to make someone feel better and happy.

- Give their emotions a name so they know what they are dealing with and recognize them in others too.

- Encourage the use of phrases like, "I am sorry" and "I hope you feel better."

Chapter 5: Manners and Following Directions

Remember those days when the boys were sent off to boarding schools? They always looked so groomed when they returned, didn't they? So knowledgeable and polished. There were many such schools in Boston and London, aimed at transforming adolescents into gracious adults. They had to abide by many strict rules, give up damaging habits and develop ones that helped them build their personality and character. Maybe you married one such adult or are one yourself. However, now that you are a parent and see your nine-year-old depicting behaviors that were considered a cardinal sin back then, you must wonder where did you fall short? Why did your child grow up this cranky, and ill-mannered?

And forget about boarding schools, we seemed to have it all under control during our childhood. Of course, we were naughty, but our level of naughty was way less. We were well-mannered, had basic etiquettes and rarely did anything to upset or embarrass our parents. Because god forbid they notice and give us the stare!

Since kids aren't born with the innate ability to learn a language, imitate behaviors and repeat actions, it has to be on us. We must have done something or not done something to raise them the way they are. If they aren't polite, it has to be on us. If they aren't disciplined and obedient, it has to be our fault, right?

Yes and no.

True, we are their first-ever teacher, we aren't the only ones they interact with. They have others they look up to, too and those influences aren't always pleasant. However, this chapter isn't aimed at making you feel bad about yourself or your parenting, it is to help you realize that it still isn't too late to make amends. They are still young and naïve and in the process of learning. So why not stem the right habits and nip the bad ones? Starting with good manners and discipline, of course!

Learning to Behave and Becoming Well-Mannered

The ability to act decent, with grace and politely is another great social skill to have. Good manners refer to the set of behaviors and actions that someone exhibits out of habit. For example, saying sorry when they hit someone, starting the question with "please" when requesting something or replying with a "thank you" when their request is fulfilled. It also involves being disciplined and not creating unnecessary chaos like crying too loud, throwing a temper tantrum, being aggressive, biting or hitting other kids, etc.

According to Faye de Muyshondt, the author of *Socialsklz :-) (Social Skills) for Success: How to Give Children the Skills They Need to Thrive in the*

Modern World, and a manners coach, good manners give children the chance to lead a happy and prosperous life. It is the classic recipe to create friends and have more opportunities to hear yes instead of nos.

Why is Good Manners and Discipline Important?

There is more than just one reason to teach your children good manners and lead their life with discipline. For starters, good manners should be a way of life. We shouldn't just teach our kids to behave well at social gatherings but teach them to act civil and responsible at all times. The best way is to begin early as a habit picked up early on is hard to let go if they are bad ones. Therefore, if they have been exposed to bad manners and a lack of discipline in the house, chances are they are going to pick up the same. This will lead them to trouble in places like schools, public events, and even weddings and restaurants. Not to mention, you will be the one to have to deal with the display of bad manners. Other than that:

Good manners or social graces help develop other social skills. Remember the time when your child was in kindergarten? Did you ever send them to school without a healthy snack or lunch? Social graces are the same. When kids who lack basic manners, go out in the world, they become a major turn-off to others, especially the kids their age. They may not mind your child taking their toy without permission, but they will start to when your child refuses to give it back or respond with hitting or biting. This example shows that your child lacks manners and everyone will be quick to point it out.

Activities to Instill Good Manners at an Early Age

By now, you must be desperately looking forward to this section, as we may have scared you a little bit. Well, worry not, these games and activities are the perfect way to teach them about something so important and yet don't make them realize that they are being schooled.

Question Time

To encourage good behavior and manners, you must first know how much work you need to do and where you need to begin with. Think of this as not a game, but rather a reality check for you as a parent. In this first exercise, you are going to ask them a series of questions to check for their responses. You start by offering them made-up scenarios and ask them to respond with "how will they deal with it." For example, how will they deal/respond:

- When someone walks in front of you?
- Ask them politely to excuse you, or,
- Push them and move forward

- When someone sits too close to them?
- Push them aside, or,
- Make room for them by moving to the other side
- When someone wants the toy you are playing with?
- Give it to them, or,
- Refuse to share or take turns
- When someone gives you something?
- Say thank you, or,
- Take it without saying thank you.

DIY Manners Box

In this activity, start with cutting a few colored printer sheets into small three-inch coins or squares. Write one good manner on each sheet of paper and place it beside an empty jar with an open slid in the lid to push the sheets inside. Tell your child to put one sheet in the jar whenever they perform the good action written on it. The examples you can write on the little sheets can be the following:

- I said, thank you
- I said sorry
- I said please
- I shared my toy with my sibling

- I changed into my night clothes myself
- I watched 1 hour of TV today
- I completed all my homework
- I knocked on the door before entering the room
- I greeted everyone when entering the house
- I covered my mouth when I sneezed/coughed
- I washed my hands before every meal
- I brushed my teeth before going to bed etc.

Set a reward if they add 5+ sheets of paper in the jar by the end of the day. You will notice how eager they will be to perform these actions. Soon, all these activities will turn into a life-long habit.

Manners Tea Party

To teach basic eating and dining out manners, invite them to a tea party to portray basic dining etiquettes. Show them how awful it looks when they run around a restaurant, smash plates, make noise and disturb others. Show them how the whole scene can be as calm and elegant.

Practice Phone Manners

Phone manners, like table or communication manners, are also important. They teach kids how to respond on the phone politely. Pretend to have a call with them, several times during the day and teach them what to say by offering them different situations. For example, you can call in to say that you are a friend of theirs and that you need to borrow their school copy as they are facing trouble with the homework. Or you can act like you are a relative that wants to talk to your mother or father. Teach them the basics first and then show them how they can improvise.

Tell them to always greet the person with a gracious greeting like, 'hello' or 'hi.' Then, ask them their name and purpose of the call like, "May I know who is calling?" or "Who do you want to speak to?" and then tell the caller to wait until you get your father/mother to the phone.

Rate Them

If you want to instill good behavior and manners in your child, you must know what intrigues them. Praises, compliments, and acknowledgment are some of the most rewarding ways to get them to do something. It is no secret that every child wishes to impress their parents. It's like a goal they have to achieve. Thus, they resort to behaviors and actions they notice you like or praise.

This activity, however, takes it up a notch. Here you not only praise them for their effort but also let others know about it. All you need is a sheet of paper with their name on it and a few stickers in the shape of a heart or stars. You make a list of chores you want them to do or behaviors you want them to demonstrate and once they do them, you give them a star right beside the chore or behavior. The more stars they get, the bigger the reward. The rewards don't have to be something tangible always. It can also be things like 15-minutes extra of TV watching or getting their favorite dessert after dinner etc.

Additional Tips and Info

Whether you believe it or not, a well-mannered child stands out for their discipline and politeness. Teaching good manners isn't hard and just a little practice and repetition of good manners does the job. Here are a few tips to get you started!

- Encourage the use of words like "please," "thank you," and "sorry."

- Set rewards for your children when they respond with politeness and exhibit good table, communication, or playing manners.

- Don't forget to boost their ego and foster repetition of certain good behavior by complimenting and praising it. They will likely do it again, just to impress you.

- When taking them someplace, let them know what is expected of them before you leave the house. Also, subtly highlight any repercussions for bad behavior such as not getting an ice-cream on the way back home if they misbehave.

- But when listing your expectations, make them age-appropriate. You can't expect them to stay seated when every other kid is having the time of their lives in the jumping castle.

Chapter 6: Making Friends and Collaborative Play

This next social skill that we are about to discuss is by far, the most rewarding and comforting in our lives. Friends are a blessing. We can come up with the weirdest of problems to them and be positive about finding a solution together. They are our support, our rock when times get tough, our ATM when we are short on cash, our mood boosters when we are down and surely, the most valuable part of our lives. They have been this one constant in our lives that never lose their charm. We got out of bed for them when we were young and still do before, going to the office. On some gloomy days, they are the only source of happiness that serves as motivation to get up from the bed and do something.

That being said, who would want to deprive their child of the same?

For our children, making friends is an important part of growing up. It is important to have someone like ourselves to develop our social and emotional skills. Through friends, we learn of attributes like self-esteem, altruism, competence, and confidence. Multiple studies suggest that having friends from an early age has a positive impact on our personalities. It helps us develop our identity to be more precise. As kids grow up together gathered by their friends, they fall less prey to the stresses in life and navigate negative challenges and emotions with a strong will and confidence.

Other than that, having friends in life:

- Positively influences our mental and physical health
- Improves our self-esteem and self-conscious
- Develops basic social skills like communication and discipline
- Improves school performance
- Increases chances to cope with mental stresses and physical transitions
- Boosts wellness ad happiness and leaves a positive outlook on life
- Encourages good behavior and manners
- Builds our problem-solving skills
- Teaches the importance of collaboration and teamwork
- Motivates to be open-minded and accept differences

Why Should Parents Encourage Collaborative Play

Also referred to as social play, collaborative play is the first step to building life-long friendships. Unlike adults, children rarely "click" and have to be introduced to one another. They have to spend time together, share their interests and passions before calling each other a friend. Luckily, the collaborative play offers them this chance to get to know each other and determine if they are a good match for each or will grow up detesting each other. (In case, the hair pulling, biting, and pushing never stops)

Collaborative play mostly involves turn-taking and sharing where one child willingly offers the other something of theirs in exchange for something they want.

Most parents struggle with getting their children to cooperate. This is quite common when a new child or sibling enters the family. The former child feels threatened and lost because they begin to feel less valued or loved. Therefore, there is a constant tug of war going on in the house and you often end up yelling, telling them to stop fighting and cooperate.

Despite not being primed for social interactions, children crave relationships, closeness, and respect. Through cooperation, they learn the art of sharing. At first, they may seem a little reluctant to share their things but with time they learn to value the person more than the thing.

Secondly, it teaches them to show respect and compassion for others. Respect is something everyone wants for themselves, but rarely do they know that the fastest way to earn respect from others is by giving it to them. Kids can learn the same through collaborative play and have this important social skill ingrained in their minds.

Unlike competitive play that preys upon other's vulnerabilities, collaborative play allows kids to learn about patience, and control their impulsiveness. This comes in handy when they grow up into beautiful adults and have to share and work in confined spaces (offices) with others.

Activities that Offer the Chance for Collaborative Play

Knowing how important this can be to encourage new friendships and teamwork, we have chosen some of the simplest activities to exercise with your kid and make learning fun.

Balloon Tennis

This requires a few supplies. The star of the show will, of course, be a balloon or two of them. Next, you will need two paint sticks, one for each partner. Glue or tape paper plates on one end of each stick to make it look like a tennis racket. Then blow up the balloon and bop it up in the air using the racket. The goal is to keep it from touching the ground. This simple activity can be compiled with some basic teaching about the importance of collaboration. Let the child know that in order to succeed and keep the balloon flying in the air, they have to work together to keep it from falling.

Treasure Hunt

The treasure hunt is an all-rounder activity for kids of all ages. It is fun, engaging and requires teamwork. If the child you are trying to teach collaboration to have other siblings, ask them to join the hunt too. You can be the judge. Divide kids into two equal teams and give each one a list of things they need to find along with some clues as to where these things could be in the house. Tasks like, find three green things in the house, five-round things, find three car toys and a book with a blue cover or something heavy to lift alone.

Once the kids are done bringing their finds, sit them down and talk about the importance of collaboration. Praise the effort of each individual player after asking them how they contributed to the win.

You Go After Me

This is ideal for more than one kid and can be a fun activity when you have kids over at your house. This is supposed to be a fun tag race where children are divided into two teams and each team has a book in their hand that they have to bring to the finish line. Each team must have at least two members as one member will have to run the half course, tag the other, and hand them the book to take it to the finish line. The more members, the more tags and book passes.

This activity teaches kids that in order to win, they have to work together towards a common goal and leave their differences behind.

Additional Tips and Info

To encourage them to make new friends, you have to provide them the opportunity of collaborative plays, it is one of the most effective ways to get them to learn about the importance of sharing and caring for others. Therefore, take note of the tips mentioned below.

- Praise an act of sharing with your child. "Remember how Sarah let you play with all her toys? That was so nice of her, wasn't it?" when your child does the same, praise more! Let them know how happy it makes you when they share their things with others.

- Encourage activities and games that require shared play or turn-taking. Before you introduce yourself into the play, let them know of your intentions. "You did great with stacking those blocks, now can I take some remaining blocks to create a tower for me?" or "Can I give you my green blocks and take red ones from you to finish building my tower, please?"

- When someone is coming over to play, talk to your child about taking turns and sharing. This prepares them mentally to be supportive and not cause a temper tantrum when one of the children decides to take something from yours without seeking permission first.

Chapter 7: Responsibility and Cooperation

Cooperation is an art form that nearly every adult exercises. It would be hard to find someone who doesn't as it sets the foundation for friendships and relationships, be it professional or personal. Therefore, it is also regarded as an essential social skill that all kids must learn to develop. Or else, the world has been known to be a harsh teacher indeed!

It is a skill that requires interaction and responsibility. It doesn't matter if you are at home, school or in a workplace, you can't live without practicing either as it establishes harmony. Like collaborative play we discussed in the chapter above, it is what maintains peace as everyone does what they are supposed to do.

If we were to define cooperation, it can be said that it is the ability to combine various energies to work for a common goal. Think of it as a stage play, where everyone has to play a small but important part to keep the story moving forward. As easy as it sounds, it can be extremely hard for some parents to instill the idea of cooperation in young kids. Why? Because it requires not only taking responsibility for your part but also involves a combination of other attributes such as respect, thoughtfulness, and honesty.

Being a parent, we all want our kids to possess these traits as we believe it is what makes them happy.

However, the reason these are hard to nurture is that kids, by birth are focused on themselves. The good news is that, like other social skills, these too can be learned with time using the fun games, exercises, activities, and tips mentioned in the latter half of this chapter.

To begin teaching young kids about cooperation, keep this in mind that most of the learning they do is by imitating you. They see what you do, listen carefully and imitate behaviors. So if they get the opportunity to see you enjoying yourself in the company of others, helping them out with the work and making happy conversations, they will want to feel the same joy you do and thus, try to copy that behavior. This means you have to be the role model they need in their lives.

The Need to Learn to Cooperate and Help Out

Some of the most astounding benefits of cooperative concepts taught early in kids are as follows:

They make for some amazing bonding times with kids their age. Some kids, out of nature, have a hard time making or becoming friends. They have trouble initiating conversations or are too shy to respond to a friendly gesture by someone else. Unlike the competitive play, where one rejoices when the other loses, cooperation allows kids to explore, discover and succeed together. Be it completing a jigsaw puzzle, building a sandcastle, or pushing one another on a swing, cooperation makes things more fun and joyful. It can serve to be a great friendship builder, something highly essential to have in today's world. It makes children see that they can count on one another. This also builds trust and compassion for one another.

Secondly, cooperation serves as a great means to learn and teach one another skills and experiences. Despite having a single goal, every child involved in the activity has to ensure that they do their part right. This means that they, themselves have a goal to accomplish which will help others finish theirs. In cooperative settings, teamwork is rewarded and not just one person's effort. Everyone's role is important and contributes to the end goal. When some kids are unable to play their part right, it is cooperation that comes in hand. The rest of the kids jump in to help and achieve the goal.

Additionally, it also leads to shared decision-making where a group of children keeps aside their differences and make decisions that benefit them as a whole. For example, if one kid has a dollar and the other has three, and they both want to buy an ice-cream costing 2 dollars each, they will both have an ice-cream cone because they both want to enjoy the tasty treats together. So they decide to collect the money and buy two creams instead of letting the partner with less money starve.

If we notice carefully, we all just want to feel safe and valued. Unfortunately, the competition gives rise to argument, feistiness, and separation. Instead of bringing people together, it pulls the best of friends and colleagues apart in professional settings. When cooperative settings are fostered and entertained, it allows for openness, safety, and honesty. One can trust the judgment of the other without feeling insecure. In children, this sets the mood for positivity and encourages support for one another.

Cooperation is free of stress as it nurtures collectively. It just seems easier to be scared with someone than alone, doesn't it? There is less pressure as one can rely on the support of the other in case things go wrong. This is most common between a child and parent relationship. If they forget to do something important, like ironing their clothes the night before school, they can trust their parents to do so.

Teaching Them to Help You with Everyday Chores

The reason kids should be taught to help out with everyday chores is that sooner or later, they will have to take responsibility for their things. It may not happen right away but one day, when they move out, they won't have trouble living on their own. When they are taught to be responsible from an early age, the habit sets and discipline finds a place in their routine. Therefore, most of the activities listed below revolve around chores and how they can help kids learn the importance of cooperation and responsibility.

Chores Management

Have chores laid out for each member of the family and post it in a list form on the fridge. These could include things like cooking, folding the laundry, dusting the furniture, emptying the pet litter box or organizing the dinner table. Deliberately add a few easily doable by the youngest member of the family whom you are trying to teach the value of cooperation and responsibility. Things like help with the car wash, take out the trash, water the plants, place washed dishes in the cabinets, etc. and make it a habit to reward the one getting the most tasks completed in a day. The reward can be anything like a chocolate bar or candy or a juice box. Start with easier chores and notice when your child starts to do them out of habit. Then move onto more complex tasks like polishing shoes, ironing clothes, washing the dishes, etc.

Time to Get Working

In this next activity, you can follow the same chores list from above or create a new one from scratch. We suggest a new one as it should contain tasks that must be completed in a set time by everyone. Also, add a few tasks that require assistance from a sibling or parent and also some that are divided into two parts like one task is folding the laundry and the other is putting it in the cupboard. Each member must be assigned one task at a time. The idea is to work together and support and help other members in the completion of their tasks. Not only will that teach them about teamwork, but it will also be a fun way to teach responsibility.

Take Turns Riding

Get toys that require collaborative effort to run. For instance, buy them toys like a wagon which has to be pulled by a thread to move forward. The kids can take turns. One can sit in the wagon and the other can pull. Then the other child gets their turn to enjoy the ride while the first one moves it forward. Such activities foster turn-taking, sharing, and trust.

Another way to go about this is by getting them toys or games that require some assistance from a parent or a sibling. For example, you can get them a puzzle or blocks set where one child stacks the blocks while the other hands it to them.

This or That?

If the goal is to nurture responsibility and collaboration, make it a habit to offer them multiple choices. "Would you like to have dinner before watching TV or after it?" "Do you want to change into your nightclothes before brushing your teeth or after brushing them?"

Notice how the child gets to decide and be in control while still adhering to both of the tasks? That's how you parent smart.

Conclusion

As parents, we often think that social skills are something our kids will naturally pick up the more they mature. This isn't true. Ask yourself this, have you never met a man or woman you wished had some more manners? Maybe they cut you off in a grocery store line or overtook your car on the highway. Maybe they lost their temper in front of you or had poor control over their emotions. Maybe they lacked basic table manners and created an orchestra of sounds while eating with a fork and spoon or maybe irked you with the way they flossed their teeth later with a tooth-picking stick. Gross, we know, right. It is in these moments that we come face-to-face with the importance of good social skills.

Believe it or not but our kids are an extension of ourselves. You may have been the most modest and well-mannered child when you were young, but if your child lacks basic etiquettes, no one is going to believe that!

Besides, if you think it is something they are going to learn on their own, then why not help them become aware of their existence. You don't have to chug them down their throat but a basic understanding of what they are and the role they play in your life is in your job description. You may not be paid more in terms of money for that, but will surely gather praises and compliments for how remarkable a parent you are to your child. Let's not forget, sometimes that is all that we need.

With that thought in mind, let's just run through the lessons rather quickly, shall we? We started with a basic definition of social skills and their types. Then we moved on to connecting the dots by finding the correlation between happiness and effective social skills. Moving forward, we discussed six of the basic social skills along with some playful activities for the parents followed by some additional tips to help them get started.

All in all, we strongly believe in the development of each and every social skill discussed in the chapters. These skills are foundational, and they set the pace for the next ones to come. Teach them these and you won't have to worry about them becoming ill-mannered, lazy, shy, inattentive, and dishonest ever again!

References

39 Communication Games and Activities for Kids, Teens, and Students. (2020, April 10). Retrieved from https://positivepsychology.com/communication-activities-adults-students/

Duncan, L. G., Greenberg, M. T., & Coatsworth, J. D. (2009). Pilot Study to Gauge Acceptability of a Mindfulness-Based, Family-Focused Preventive Intervention. The Journal of Primary Prevention, 605–618.

Fox, I. (n.d.). Teaching Kids to Mind Their Manners: How to Raise a Polite Child. Retrieved from https://www.parents.com/toddlers-preschoolers/development/manners/teaching-kids-to-mind-their-manners/

How to Help Your Child Develop Empathy. (n.d.). Retrieved from https://www.zerotothree.org/resources/5-how-to-help-your-child-develop-empathy

Jones, D. E., Greenburg, M., & Crowley, M. (2015, July 28). Early Social-Emotional Functioning and Public Health: The Relationship Between Kindergarten Social Competence and Future Wellness. American Journal of Public Health, 2283-2290.

Killingsworth, M. A., & Gilbert, D. T. (2010). A Wandering Mind Is an Unhappy Mind. Science, 932.

Manyika, J., Chui, M., Merimadi, M., Bughin, J., Willmont, P., George, K., & Dewhurst, M. (2017). Harnessing automation for a future that works. McKinsey Global Institute.

Marchand, W. (2012). Depression and Bipolar Disorder: Your Guide to Recovery. Boulder: Bull Publishing Company.

Marschel, L. (2019, May 28). Emotions Discovery Bottles Inspired By Disney's Inside Out. Retrieved from Laly Mom: https://lalymom.com/emotions-discovery-bottles-inspired-by-disneys-inside-out/

Morin, A. (2019, September 13). 5 Ways to Teach Kids Old-Fashioned Manners in Today's World. Retrieved from https://www.verywellfamily.com/ways-to-teach-kids-old-fashioned-manners-in-todays-world-1094897

Morin, A. (2020, April 9). 7 Social Skills You Should Start Teaching Your Child Now. Retrieved from https://www.verywellfamily.com/seven-social-skills-for-kids-4589865

Mrazek, M. D., Franklin, M. S., Phillips, D. T., Baird, B., & Schooler, J. W. (2013). Mindfulness Training Improves Working Memory Capacity and GRE Performance While Reducing Mind Wandering. Psychological Science, 776–781.

Sanger, K. L., & Dorjee, D. (2015). Mindfulness training for adolescents: A neurodevelopmental perspective on investigating modifications in attention and emotion regulation using event-related brain potentials. Cognitive, affective & behavioral neuroscience, 696–711.

The Importance of Developing Listening and Attention Skills in Children. (2016, May 3). Retrieved from https://www.education.gov.gy/web/index.php/parenting-tips/item/1962-the-importance-of-developing-listening-and-attention-skills-in-children

Why teaching children empathy is more important than ever. (2018, February 22). Retrieved from https://www.goodstart.org.au/news-and-advice/february-2018/why-teaching-children-empathy-is-important

HOW PARENTS CAN TEACH CHILDREN TO LIVE WITH TRANSPARENCY

A Whole Heart Approach to Effectively Raising Honest and Candid Kids Without Secrets

FRANK DIXON

© **Copyright 2020 - All rights reserved.**

The content contained within this book may not be reproduced, duplicated or transmitted without direct written permission from the author or the publisher.

Under no circumstances will any blame or legal responsibility be held against the publisher, or author, for any damages, reparation, or monetary loss due to the information contained within this book, either directly or indirectly.

<u>Legal Notice:</u>

This book is copyright protected. It is only for personal use. You cannot amend, distribute, sell, use, quote or paraphrase any part, or the content within this book, without the consent of the author or publisher.

<u>Disclaimer Notice:</u>

Please note the information contained within this document is for educational and entertainment purposes only. All effort has been executed to present accurate, up to date, reliable, complete information. No warranties of any kind are declared or implied. Readers acknowledge that the author is not engaged in the rendering of legal, financial, medical or professional advice. The content within this book has been derived from various sources. Please consult a licensed professional before attempting any techniques outlined in this book.

By reading this document, the reader agrees that under no circumstances is the author responsible for any losses, direct or indirect, that are incurred as a result of the use of the information contained within this document, including, but not limited to, errors, omissions, or inaccuracies.

Introduction

A decade ago, raising sensible, good, and practical kids was rather straightforward. But not today, at least not in this age of rapid connectivity and the internet. With nearly everyone having a Wi-Fi router in their homes and 4G data packages on phones, the way we raise kids and talk to them about healthy values has changed. But this exposure has also opened new opportunities for parents to learn and reach out to expert advice and seek professional help when facing problems with their kids' upbringing. Kids, too, have started to be more inquisitive than before. But being a double-edged sword, we still need to figure out if the pros outweigh the cons when it comes to increased internet access. The dark side, of course, includes easy access to obscenity and trigger-causing information which can lead to gadget addiction.

To say the least, the role of the parents is to be ever vigilant and keep a keen eye on what the child is viewing and taking in before they are drawn to some dark cesspool. Why?

Because children begin to lie and hide things. They lie about where they were, who they were with, what they were doing, and what they plan to do next. They keep secrets and do things that their parents would otherwise tell them not to. This lack of transparency in the parent-child relationship can turn into a lifelong habit and make things uncomfortable between the two of you. You want them to open up with you, share their thoughts and ideas, not fear coming to you when they want to confess something.

Children must be taught about the repercussions their sneaking and dishonesty can have in order to discourage the forming of these habits.

Honest and open conversations about anything and everything is the way to tackle this. Having worked with families who wished they had spent more time with their kids getting to know them better, it is easy to look at the prevalent problem. Parents in their old age regret not having a household that encouraged open dialogues because their children left the nest the minute they turned 16. With more than 76 million American baby boomers looking to retire, it is time we start having this conversation and talking about the importance of good and healthy family structures and what they look like.

If you still resist the idea, you must be ready for the consequences. Little to no openness can lead to misunderstandings between the child and the parents, where the parent feels insignificant and the child feels that the parent doesn't care enough. Parenting has to be a partnership where families thrive by coming closer, addressing critical issues, and making decisions that benefit everyone equally.

It all starts with being honest and transparent. This is what the general idea of the book is about. We want parents to teach their kids to be more open and honest. We want to help them understand why children sometimes lie. We also want to pinpoint the grave mistakes they make intentionally or unintentionally which lead to children lying and being secretive.

So, without further ado, let's kick this off with the first aspect of transparency: honesty and integrity.

Chapter 1: Being Honest – Is It Important?

What does being transparent really mean? Does it mean telling the whole world about all that you do or don't do? Does it mean being honest at all times, even when it hurts to hear the truth? Does it mean having no secrets to keep or share with someone?

We believe it means trying our best not to lie about or hide information and actions that prevent the forming of a healthy relationship. We are already living in a world where nothing holds more importance than honest relationships, but even when living under the same roof, we still struggle with winning someone's trust. Ask yourself this: as a parent, do you trust that your child can do no wrong? Maybe you like to think so, but can you be certain about all their actions and behaviors behind closed doors or when you aren't with them? Can you vouch for them being honest with you 100% of the time? Can you say the same for yourself? Are you being honest when you make up lies to skip brunch with your friends or lie to your wife about getting drinks with your office colleagues?

There is nothing to be ashamed of as it is in our nature to lie, but that certainly doesn't mean you allow yourself or your kids to get away with it. As humans, we are afraid of being mistreated, misjudged, or rejected. So we trick ourselves into lying and getting away with things. We wear a mask to please everyone. We hide who we really are. So do our kids!

But what if we were to tell you that being transparent was the way out of all this?

Being transparent allows us to stay stress-free. When you are open with someone, there is little worry in your mind. When you have clear intentions about something and are willing to expose yourself and your feelings, you allow others to see the real you. There are less unpleasant surprises when we are honest and things go well for everyone. When you are transparent, you can't be manipulated. Your intentions become straightforward and there is little secrecy involved.

Despite these benefits, you will be shocked to know that we, including the kids, lie on average one to six times per day. And if we are having a conversation of approximately ten minutes, we are sure to lie at least two times during it (Feldman, 2002).

But do we really need to deceive or tell half-truths as often as we do?

According to a research study from the University of Chicago, people are much better at handling the truth than we think or credit them for (Levine & Cohen, 2018). Initially, they may act surprised or even hurt, but it is less hurt that is experienced when they find out the truth later. We do the same with our kids. To keep them safe or out of harm's way, we lie to them instead of having open conversations. We assume they won't take the truth well or be bad at taking critical feedback, but that isn't always the truth. In the research, the authors asked respondents to be completely honest with a close relation and monitored their reactions. Keep in mind, the conversations were anything but comfortable and involved several sensitive and personal questions. Many questions resulted in negative feedback, but the findings revealed that the receiver seemed okay with the truth.

Keeping this in mind, it is safe to suggest that speaking the truth and not hiding or manipulating it is the best policy.

Honesty and Wellbeing

Presented at the American Psychological Association's 120th annual convention, this brief study led by Anita E. Kelly, a psychology professor at the University of Notre Dame suggested that on average, Americans tell approximately 11 lies per week (Kelly, 2012). She, along with her fellow researchers wanted to study if telling fewer lies resulted in improved health or not.

The study consisted of about 110 people, 34% adults and 66% college students. Their ages ranged from 18 to 71. The participants were divided into two groups: one of them was asked to make an effort to stop lying for the next ten weeks, while the others weren't. Each week, both groups were called in for a polygraph test to determine how many lies they told during the week. Some tests related to their health and wellbeing were also conducted. Participants in the no-lie group reported that what caused them to stop lying over the weeks was the avoidance of fake excuses and exaggerations. They told the researchers that whenever they felt like lying as a response to some questions asked by someone, they resorted to asking a different question in return. After studying their test results and comparing them with the results of the second group, researchers were able to notice a significant change in their health comparisons. The first group seemed to have improved their health throughout the 10-weeks experiment. This was evident by looking at their stress levels, which showed a major decline. They also reported fewer headaches and sore throats.

This study provides enough evidence to believe that being truthful, honest, and transparent is what helps keep our health in check. It prevents us from feeling stressed, anxious, or nervous – responses that are triggered when we tell a lie.

Honesty Reduces Stress

In the magazine Shape, Dr. Arthur Markman reports that every time we tell a lie, our nervous system releases the stress hormone cortisol into our brain (Heid, n.d.). Cortisol sets in motion our immune system, which starts fighting against this imbalance in the brain. The more lies we tell to keep up with the first one, the more cortisol is released. Anxiety takes over and we become stressed. If left untreated, this can lead to other medical and emotional issues like irritation, and anger. Since we don't want to get caught, we keep adding onto the first lie to save ourselves from embarrassment, without realizing the harmful effects lying has on our brain, body, and mood.

Those who often find themselves lying to get away with something or cover up for a mistake also report anxiety in the form of a worn-out immune system, headaches, heart palpitations, insomnia, and dizziness. It is easy enough to recognize the reasons behind why many middle-aged people face heart-related issues today. The added pressure of work, increasing competition, and high expectations that compels one to lie. But our kids don't need that, and we can prevent this from becoming their future reality by teaching them the right values and ethics, which includes being transparent.

Honesty and Future Success

It doesn't matter if our kids have just started to walk or asked for a car as their graduation present, we want them to have the best of everything. We want them to be better than who we were as kids and do better than we ever did. We want them to succeed, follow their passions, and live life as freely as they can.

What if we told you that all of this is possible if you just teach them good values and high morals?

Being honest and transparent cuts through the red tape, it minimizes frustrations and distractions, and it eliminates indecisiveness. When we are honest with ourselves and others, we move faster towards our goals because our intent and conscience are clear. We live the way we feel. There is little to no disguise when it comes to speaking about our plans and working towards them. We don't expect our children to know what they really want from the minute they step into this world, but clarity will help them make the right decisions, beneficial to them.

Honest actions and speech gain the attention of others and that goes for professionals too. No manager or employer would want to hire a dishonest employee that hides behind lies to conceal their mistakes. They also wouldn't want to hire someone who has a bad reputation. Everyone, including employers, want to be influenced by someone that holds honesty and transparency important. It is no secret that good ethics and moral conduct are the fundamental components of professional success. Being honest is more than just following all the rules and regulations. It is about having values and principles that make you an example for others

Think about this: if you raise a child who is dishonest and lacks integrity, no one would like to be their friend. When they eventually step into the professional field, none of their colleagues will trust them; no one will appreciate an employee that lies, claims credit for the work of others, steals office supplies, and makes up a lie to prove themselves innocent after getting caught. Right now, these may not seem like BIG things to you but let us remind you that these seemingly insignificant things add up over time and can ruin a reputation.

This is why you have to start today. Not only will being honest and transparent save your little one embarrassment and shame, but it will also improve their long term prospects and wellbeing.

Chapter 2: Lies, Lies, and More Lies...

Ever wondered how easy it would be to spot a lie if our noses started to grow like Pinocchio's? We would notice the second our kids lied to us. But then, it would also be harder to parent them as we lie to them too. Yes, the cookie jar wasn't stolen by thieves and their favorite blanket isn't in the wash.

In this chapter, we explore the world of lying in detail. We will discuss the many different types of lies and liars, and we will debate whether lying can EVER be a good thing and in what conditions it is considered acceptable, if at all.

But first, what does lying mean? According to the dictionary, lying refers to making a false statement. However, that is not enough for us to work with. The reason we can't simply define what qualifies as a lie and what doesn't is because there is an issue involving intent and expectation. For starters, no one just casually lies. No one casually offers a misleading answer to a question. There has to be some form of motivation involved.

To grasp the concept of lying better, we need to take a look at the types of liars as well as the types of lies kids in particular resort to, to determine if all lying is bad or if it can be good – if the intention is justifiable.

The Many Faces of Liars

As believed, liars can be of different types. Children usually don't know the difference between the depths of the lie they are telling but as a parent, you must know.

- White Liars: liars who have a habit of hiding things or telling half-truth are white liars. They lie because they assume they are protecting someone from harm. This involves a child telling you that the food you cooked for them is delicious because they want a favor from you. This type of lying is more akin to sugar-coating, so it can be let go if it occurs occasionally.

- Occasional Liars: as the name suggests, kids who lie infrequently are occasional liars. Occasional liars actually have the habit of eventually confessing to their lies or the wrong they did which resulted in them telling a lie. They are quick to seek forgiveness and show a willingness to work on themselves to prevent it from happening again. They confess because they are overcome by guilt and can't keep quiet.

- Careless Liars: liars who don't care about how many times they have lied or about the severity and consequences of their lies. They are masters of twisted stories and thus aren't very reliable. For example, it is that kid in class who brags about going on luxury yacht trips every summer when in reality they just spend it visiting grandma. They never confess to their lies even when confronted and will tell more to cover up the previous ones.

- Compulsive Liars: these are the worst kind of liars, who lie out of habit. Every word out of their mouth is inconsistent and they prefer lying over telling the truth. Since habits are formed after repeated action or behavior, many people believe that adult compulsive liars may have had traumatic or problematic childhoods, where lying may have been a necessity.

Types of Lies Most Children Concoct

Now that we have identified the types of liars, we can move on to looking at the types of lies told most commonly by kids and teenagers.

We have *imaginary lies* where the child, due to poor comprehension about what is real and what isn't, exaggerated a scenario to seek attention. For instance, your child talking about how their toys move at night after everyone goes to bed.

Then come *need-based lies*, which are most common with kids aged between three to five. Need-based lies involve emotional manipulation so that the children can get something they want. For example, a child complaining about pain in their arm to avoid doing their chores in the house.

Thirdly, we have *social lies*, often spoken when someone doesn't want to engage socially. It is a child asking to skip school because their tummy hurts on the day of a big test or presentation.

There are also *routine lies*, where the child just can't control themselves from telling a lie. Routine lying can develop into *pathological lying*, which can point to a personality disorder and thus should be discussed with a child specialist or therapist.

Fear-based lies are lies spoken out of fear or danger of being caught or punished. These are mostly spoken when the child has done something they know to be wrong and wants to cover it up. They don't want to be punished and resort to telling a lie.

And finally, we have *admirable lies* where children exaggerate about their qualifications, skills, or successes to impress others. An example of this would be a child joining a new school and telling everybody about his extra-curricular skills in an exaggerated manner.

Can Lying be a Good Thing?

As parents, we want our kids to never lie. We think that honesty is a moral imperative and we are keen on instilling it as a belief in our children. Besides, we have all read *The Boy Who Cried Wolf* and *Pinocchio*. We see kids who lie as primed for trouble in the future. But what if we told you that they were smarter and more vigilant?

According to some scientists, lying among children is a sign of intelligence. We already know that kids learn to lie by the time they turn two. They have been lying before then too, but once they turn two, they start to lie because they see lying as a means of getting what they want.

In an experiment conducted in the mid-1980s, a team of researchers led by developmental psychologist Michael Lewis set out to find out how easily kids lie and how easy it is for adults to recognize the lie. They would ask a child in a room to NOT peek at the toy hidden behind them in the room; the researcher would then leave the room after making an excuse. Approximately 80% of the children looked at the toy within seconds of the researcher leaving the room. When the researcher returned and asked the kids if they had taken a peek, many of them lied about it. What the kids didn't know was that they were being recorded throughout the experiment. When they lied, their response and expressions were recorded too. The footage of the second half of the experiment was shown to social workers, police officers, primary school teachers, and even judges, who were asked to spot the liars but couldn't. Finally, the parents of the kids were called upon but even they were unable to detect the lie.

The kids who had lied about not peeking at the toy showed a higher verbal IQ than those who didn't lie, and the kids who didn't peek at the toy at all had the highest IQ.

As interesting as this is, it doesn't mean that lying should be celebrated. It is still a negative habit and your child should keep at a distance from it. Lying should only be acceptable when it is aimed to spare someone from hurt, fear, or trouble. Meaning, you can't make your child tell that truth about the meatloaf Aunt Julie served at Christmas. Imagine your kid telling her that it was so bad that even your dog refused to eat it. Would that be okay?

Besides, we have been lying to our kids for years. If they still believe in an old guy bringing them presents once a year, you have been lying to them. Even you know why you do it and why it is considered acceptable.

Make it a point to teach your children what kind of lying is acceptable, when the lie is to prevent hurt or fear in others, especially those we care about like our family and friends.

Chapter 3: Preventing the Habit of Lying

Now that we understand the basics of lying and the different types of lies and liars, the next important step is the identification of whether you are raising a child who is a liar or not. Again, keep in mind that this section isn't to demean or judge your capacity as a parent: there's just a problem that needs to be addressed and some work to counter it.

Although it can be almost impossible to detect a good lie, there are still some signs useful for spotting a liar, especially a child or a teenager, who is still learning to lie. It may take you some practice to notice these in the beginning but the more you notice, the clearer they will become. Once you have spotted a lie, no need to yell at the child. There are various ways to handle it, which we will discuss later in this chapter.

Signs I am Raising a Liar

Here's what you need to look out for when trying to catch a lying child.

- They take long pauses before answering: this suggests there is some thinking going on which involves concocting a story to tell. When they are speaking the truth, they already know all the facts and don't need to think or pause before answering. Pauses indicate they are hiding something.

- They change the subject or try to keep their sentences short. When asked a question, they will either try to avoid it completely by going off-topic or tell only a fraction of the truth. For instance, if you asked them if they went to the library after school, they might respond with something like, "Hey do you know there was a guest at school today?" Notice how they haven't really answered the question and just stated a loosely connected fact.

- Their pitch changes. When someone tries to lie, a difference in their vocal pitch can be observed. Their answers will seem hasty, loud, or uttered with a stutter. It is most common with occasional liars as they start to feel guilty.

- They talk faster. Remember the first sign? It suggested that when someone lies, they usually take long pauses between questions. But lack of silence or speaking faster than normal is also a sign of lying. When kids and teenagers begin to talk quickly when they normally don't communicate in that manner, it can also be a sign that they are trying hard to convince you of something.

- Their eye movement changes: liars mostly avoid eye contact. This is also a sign to look for if they are consistently avoiding looking you in the eyes and are looking down.

Why Do Kids Lie?

Lying is rather common among adolescents and teenagers. According to one study, 96% of kids lie at home at one point or another. The study also classified the number of lies based on the ages of the children. For instance, it was found that kids aged four and five lie every two hours, whereas kids aged six and older lie every hour on average. If this is true, they are lying to us at least five to six times per day, which is shocking.

No one wants their kids to be liars. However, this isn't the real worry we are going to address here. The real worry is this: why do kids lie? What motivates them to resort to dishonesty? Why do they hide the truth? Researchers believe one or more of these reasons are to blame.

They may not know they are lying as they are too young to distinguish between reality and imagination. They are simply making up tales to make routine tasks seem interesting.

Secondly, it seems like a new thing they have just been introduced to and are testing out the behavior. They have seen it work and are excited to be using it often. Maybe it has kept them safe from punishment or impressed their parents, so they see it as a rewarding behavior.

Another reason is to make themselves seem impressive, talented, or to inflate their self-esteem. This is most common among kids suffering from a lack of confidence. They exaggerate and tell lies. They lie to gain the approval of others and to boost their self-esteem when they get away with it. Lies make them appear smarter and special in the eyes of others – something that they love and crave.

A child may also lie to avoid getting in trouble or avoid doing something unpleasant. When this is the case, it is important to note the trigger and focus on that instead of lecturing the child about the danger of lying.

Another reason to lie is out of fear or when kids want to take the focus off themselves. For example, if a kid is shy and doesn't like to attend big gatherings, they may make up excuses to skip them and stay at home instead.

Kids who want to be accepted by their parents, peers, and friends also lie sometimes. According to one study, when kids feel that they won't be able to live up to the standards and expectations set by their parents, they lie about reaching them to avoid punishment and shame (Smith & Rizzo, 2017). They know if they tell the truth, they will be held accountable for falling short, but if they lie, they might avoid getting in trouble. During the research, kids aged four to nine were given two stories to read. Each story had the main character doing something bad and lying about it. In the first story, the main character stole candy from a buddy, and in the second, they pushed another kid from a swing. Half the kids read the stories where the candy-stealer confessed about their wrongdoing to their mothers and the swing-pusher lied. The other half read the stories where the candy-stealer lied and the swing-pusher confessed to the crime.

Throughout the reading session, the researchers kept asking the kids what they thought of the main character and of their crime.

At the same time, the researchers also called in the parents of those children and presented them with a questionnaire asking them to rate their child's lying behavior. The questionnaire included questions such as: "Do they confess to a crime?", "Do they seem impatient or out of character when lying?" etc.

The children whose parents rated them better at telling the truth were also the same that suggested that the main character would feel much better if they came clean with their parents about their crime. These findings suggest that children are honest when they think it pleases their parents.

The Dangers of Lying

When kids develop a taste for lying because their lying saved them from their parents, they form a pattern. This is highly dangerous as it is hard to get rid of a bad habit, especially when the kid is growing up and argues about everything. They present you with all the excuses in the world as to why they lied in the first place without being sorry or ashamed. This breaks the trust in the relationship as it becomes harder for you to believe them, even when they aren't lying.

So, when you are trying to sit them down and talk to them about it, don't forget about the dangers mentioned below.

It Isn't Good for Their Health

We already know how lying adds to stress in the body which can lead to anxiety. As a parent, you want to do anything you can to prevent your children from developing any health issues.

Things Will Only Get More Complicated

It would be much easier if we lied about something just once and everyone forgot about it, but a lie always comes back to bite us. And then, we have to tell more lies and then more lies to cover up for the second batch of lies. The cycle never stops – unless we come clean about it.

You Lose All Trust in the Eyes of Others

An honest person is respected by everyone. A dishonest person isn't. People stop trusting you or your word. Your value declines in their eyes and no matter what you do, they will always see a liar in you and avoid being close to you or rely on you for anything. If this isn't punishment enough, we don't know what is.

It Is a Lot of Work

No one ever said that lying was supposed to be the easy way out. True, it might have kept your child out of trouble once or twice, but it needs a lot of work. There is so much to remember and it can be hard to recall as isn't natural. Imagine if you told your boss that you were sick and thus didn't show up to work once and then when asked about it again the next month, you failed to remember and make up another lie instead? What are the chances you will get away with it? What if you get caught? Are you willing to lose your self-respect for something as little as this? Let your child know that another danger of lying is that you have to keep up with the same story. If there are any inconsistencies, their chances of being caught increase.

Others Feel Devalued

When you are caught lying to someone, it is telling them that you don't value them enough to come clean. Where does that leave the relationship, be it between a parent and a child, a child and their friends, or a child and their peers and teachers?

Lying Can Turn Into a Bad Habit Hard to Get Rid Of

Once the child starts to lie, it can be really hard to stop. It is like an addiction: the more you lie and get away with them, the more power it gives you. If you develop a taste for it, you will eventually turn into a pathological liar that lies about everything without a reason or cause. According to one study, the more we lie, the easier it becomes, and the more frequently we speak the truth, the harder lying becomes (Verschuere, Spruyt, Meijer, & Otgaar, 2010).

There Is Little Sense of Accomplishment

When we lie, we deprive ourselves of feelings of accomplishment, even if our lie succeeds. Triumph originating from a lie is short-lived and filled with self-contempt and guilt. The victory seems hollow and does little to boost our self-esteem in the long run. It even undermines our self-image.

And Finally, Lies Can Mislead

If you have told someone a lie, an image of the event or story you concocted sets in their mind. They start believing it to be the truth and get misled. For instance, if a child tells their parents that they have finished their homework, they might plan a night out for fun. But when they find out that the child lied, it will break their heart.

Chapter 4: Ssshh, Don't Tell My Parents!

All kids hide the truth or keep secrets. Even when they are honest most of the time, there are still things that they like to keep from their parents. As they grow up, they figure out what behaviors get them reward and praises, and what gets them in trouble. Since the temptation of the things that end up in arguments or punishments is bigger, they continue to attempt them without letting anyone know.

In this chapter, we discuss the many reasons why kids, especially teenagers, lie to their parents and keep secrets. But first, let's make one thing clear – are secrecy and privacy the same? Or are they the two sides of the same coin?

Secrecy Isn't Privacy

In the words of Dr. Laura Schlessinger, privacy means withholding information that isn't of concern to someone. Its disclosure won't impact others and keeping it to yourself won't affect or harm a parent or partner. Secrecy, on the other hand, is withholding information that directly affects the wellbeing of a parent or partner and can have a detrimental effect. Thus, privacy is acceptable, and secrecy isn't.

To understand it in simpler terms, privacy involves inobservance. For example, you take a bath. This is something you can keep private. It is something that concerns no one but you. The same applies to our dreams and fantasies. They are ours to share or not share with someone because it won't make a big difference in their lives. It is solely on you to decide when to share or if, to share it with someone. For example, you can choose to keep your passion for playing the piano from your child. You can spend your whole life keeping that secret, or you can decide to share it with them.

Secrecy involves hiding. It isn't the same as privacy and it stems from a deliberate effort to keep something in the dark. Secrecy has the potential to negatively impact the lives of others. When such secrets are revealed, they can create feelings of insecurity, betrayal, and hurt. An example of this would be you hiding from your kids that they were adopted or that they have other siblings.

Why Do Kids Prefer Secrecy?

In a PBS Frontline Special in 1999 titled *The Lost Children of Rockdale County*, the narrators told a story about a syphilis outbreak in a wealthy suburb in Atlanta. After evaluating the cases, the health officials reported that the majority of the affected were teenagers, some as young as thirteen years old. Further investigation revealed that some teenagers had more than one sexual partner, with some having dozens and being engaged in all sorts of risky sexual activities. Even more shocking was that these kids didn't come from broken families and neither were they abused or homeless. Most of them were from typical families. The parents were completely unaware of their kids being involved in sexual activities at all.

The reason this story is important here is that most of the teens suffering from syphilis knew that there was something wrong with them but kept it a secret. This suggests that kids, especially teens have a world of their own that excludes anyone that isn't their age or a friend. Their secret lives are the result of a longing to be a part of a cult and do things that make them seem cool – things that their parents would never approve of.

Other than that, kids also hide things out of shame and guilt, especially when they have been hurt in one form or the other. For example, they will hide sexual assault or bullying from their parents or elder siblings because they feel they are somehow to blame for what happened to them.

They may also be afraid of your reaction. Households where communication only happens over the dinner table are spaces where secrets are the most common. The lack of communication and support from the parents teaches the child to stay quiet, because they have either been scolded when they come clean about something, had to give up their gadgets, or were grounded for it. None of these prospects are appealing to a teenager, so they keep quiet.

And finally, there is disapproval and disappointment that kids don't want their parents to feel towards them. So, they change their grades from a 'D' to an 'A' on their report card.

Things My Child Doesn't Want Me to Know

Now that we understand the motivations behind secrecy, it is time to note the many lies or secrets they will tell or keep from you whether you believe it or not. Some people who tend to be rather open and communicative with their kids are shocked when they find out that their children have been hiding things from them. It is only a matter of time before you find lingerie you didn't buy them or a packet of cigarettes in their coat.

Here's what they will hide from you 90% of the time.

They Are Friends With People You Don't Approve Of

As parents, it isn't hard for us to spot which friends are keepers and which aren't. Call it a sixth sense, but we get a bad feeling about some of their friends. But here's the thing: despite you telling your kid to stay away from them for their own good, they are going to stay friends with them. They may not meet in the open like before, but they will stay in touch.

They Are on Social Platforms You Can't Track

Platforms like Facebook and Twitter are for old people now as there isn't much secrecy left, so kids are getting smarter in their choices of social media to keep their secrecy. They are signing up on platforms that keep their identity hidden or that are too complicated to be understood by a parent. You can never fully know what they are up to online.

They Are or Trying to Be Sexually Active

We have all lived through puberty when hormones start doing their thing. If your child, who is in their teens, isn't sexually active, they are trying to be. It is best to have the dreaded talk about protection and being safe sooner rather than later.

They Are Lying About Sleepovers

Have their sleepovers increased in the past few months? Do you always feel like they overdress a little to go to a sleepover? Chances are they are sneaking off to places they don't want you to find out about because you won't approve of them. This is a common secret among teenagers. They are always looking for excuses to party and be in places they aren't supposed to be in.

What Secrets Are Okay to Keep and What Aren't?

Keeping in mind the many secrets they may have been keeping from you, it is good to discuss what are good and bad secrets. Research suggests that kids often hide big secrets like assault or rape from their parents because they don't want to be viewed differently and they just want the thing to go away. However, as parents, it is our biggest fear that something bad will happen to our children and we won't be able to stop it. It is a proactive and sensible approach to know the difference between what secrets are acceptable and what aren't.

Secrets that are safe to keep

- Gossip about friends and family that are too petty to be disclosed in the open or that won't hurt them in some way.

- Surprised birthday parties organized for someone close to you as long as they don't violate someone's privacy.

- Information about gifts, which will be opened at a certain date or time and will no longer remain a secret then.

- Fun games as long as they are safe to play without supervision and don't involve harming someone's life.

Secrets that are unsafe to keep

- Being touched inappropriately, even if by a parent.

- Games that may harm someone or ruin their life.

- Photos or videos of someone that would otherwise be considered obscene or pornographic.

- The request for favors from someone that aren't appropriate in exchange for a gift or favor.

- Gossip about someone's sexuality or life that would ruin their reputation.

- Anything that bothers you enough that you can't get your head around it.

Chapter 5: What Am I Doing Wrong?

Now that we are aware of their motives and the things they keep from us, it is best to develop and establish an understanding with the children to involve you in their plans and share with you more. They must, at all times, know that they can come to you with their problems and worries. When they know that they will be listened to and valued, they will feel more comfortable sharing and opening up.

However, when parents try to do this, they often cross the line between being supportive and become invasive. Instead of becoming active listeners, they try to 'fix' the issues for them. The emphasis should be on trying to hear them, rather than problem-solve for them. Once we learn the difference between the two, it will be much easier to communicate without reacting to the things they tell you.

To better highlight the mistakes you might be making, below are some things you need to take note of and try your best not to resort to them.

Mistakes Parents Make When Struggling to Prevent Secrecy

For starters, they themselves teach kids to keep secrets. When was the last time you told your child to keep a secret for you? Was it when you two baked a cake for daddy on his birthday and didn't tell him until he got back home? Were you not the one to encourage them to lie for you when they talked to their dad on the phone? The more frequently you expect your children to lie on your behalf or share only half-truths, the more they will see it as a good thing. It is okay to have a few secrets every now and then don't make it a habit. As a parent, the first mistake you make is teaching your children to lie for you. Other than that:

Expecting Them to Keep Secrets

Kids are naïve and forgetful. You may have told them to keep a secret but even you know they are quick to open their mouth and let it all out. So, to add an extra layer of protection over your secret, you bribe them to stay true to their end of the bargain. "If you don't tell this to anyone, I will take you to the mall tomorrow and you can get a toy."

And there is the second mistake. You gave them a strong motive to keep their mouth shut, which is also telling them that if someone offers something of value in return, it is best to keep quiet. The reason this mistake is so serious is that groomers and pedophiles use these tactics when preying on children. They tell them to stay quiet about what goes on between them in exchange for a bag of chocolates or candies. Now, since you have been doing the same with your child i.e. bribing them with goods and things of their interest, they assume this is how things work and stay quiet. You can imagine the rest yourself.

Being Dishonest

Another mistake parents make is giving kids their impression that lying is an acceptable trait. If they see you lying, they will think that it is okay to hide things or lie about them because mommy and daddy do it too. So, the next time you make up an excuse about having a headache and skipping work or lying on the phone to some friend, make sure your child isn't in the same room as you. Of course, you may have your reasons to lie, but don't do it in front of the kids.

Not Speaking of the Dangers of Lying

Every parent has to sit down with their children and talk about the dangers of secrecy and lying. If you haven't done that already and they are still unable to make the connection between good and bad lies, then you are at fault here, not them. So, the next time they hide stuff, it's on you, not them!

Not Talking About the Repercussions of Lying

Sadly, not many parents recognize the repercussions secrecy can have. We have all seen TV shows and movies where teenagers hide rape and assault they witnessed but kept quiet to save themselves from being expelled or getting grounded by their parents. There have been cases where children lied to their parents to go to a party and ended up drunk-driving and injuring pedestrians. Not telling your children about how grave the consequence of secrecy can be is a serious mistake that could end up putting them in danger.

Refusing to Punish the Child Over Lying

If your children have been caught sneaking and hiding things from you, not punishing them for it gives them the impression that is okay to lie and keep secrets. How else will they get over a bad habit if you continue to act normal about it? They must be disciplined, if not punished, to prevent them from keeping secrets in the future.

Effective Ways to Prevent Secrecy

Now that we are aware of the dangers of secrecy and the mistakes many parents unintentionally make, how do we put an end to it? How do we teach our kids to stop keeping secrets and nip the habit in the bud? Here are a few workable strategies to apply.

Teach Them About Safe and Unsafe Secrets

The first step to preventing secrecy and encouraging transparency is teaching your children the difference between the two so that they are clearly aware of what is good and acceptable and what is bad and unacceptable. When they are able to make the distinction, they will less likely to be quiet about unsafe or bad secrets.

Discuss Daily Routines and Activities

Find a suitable time to have a detailed chat about how their day went, what they did, and who they engaged with. Ask them about their friends and teachers and how they feel about them. Inquire if they are happy at school and not hiding something unsafe or bad from you. Be calm while doing so or else the child will feel like you are violating their privacy.

Win Their Trust

All kids, big or small, crave space. The best way to provide them with it and still be sure nothing suspicious goes on without your knowledge is by gaining their trust and confidence. If they come to you to gossip about someone and tell you strictly to not share it with anyone as it is confidential, then value that! Don't go behind their back telling the whole world about it, because when they find out, they will no longer trust you.

Be an Active Listener

Sometimes, kids just want to be heard by someone so that they can voice their concerns and worries. When your child comes to you with confidence that you will offer some advice, use that time to talk to them, rather than disciplining or lecturing them, especially when they have made a mistake and are feeling guilty about it. This is the time to let them know that they have your undying support and to encourage them to come up with a way to rectify the situation.

Chapter 6: Encouraging Openness

Ever seen a caterpillar going through the various stages of metamorphosis to grow into a beautiful butterfly? Kids grow up in the same manner. With good values, high morals, and effective, healthy communication binding the whole family together, they become the best versions of themselves.

But the transition isn't sudden. There are many challenges along the way, mental and physical barriers that endanger the process of becoming independent, emotionally intelligent, and confident.

It is no secret that healthy relationships are only possible when healthy communication prevails. There are instances where the parent-child relationship suffers because of poor communication or misunderstandings. To prevent distance and rift in relationships, it is important that parents ensure openness towards the ideas and thoughts of their children so that they don't leave anything out when confiding in you.

In this chapter, we will discuss the role of family conversations and how they can minimize the habit of lying and secrecy in kids.

Importance of Healthy Communication

Spoken communication is the essence of the relationship between you and your child. It is highly unlikely that kids brought up in households where communication isn't valued or happens infrequently will grow up to become strong, confident, and self-reliant individuals. They go on to lead lives lacking love and compassion and have a hard time building meaningful relationships with their partners and friends.

Conversely, when communication is common and happens every day, children learn about the world and how it works from the experience of their parents. They are able to be expressive, open up, and share their thoughts and feelings without ever feeling awkward.

But can it also prevent lying and secrecy?

If you are looking for a short answer then YES, IT CAN!

If we go back and look at the reasons for lying and secret-keeping, we notice that both of them arise from a form of fear. The children fear being punished or causing disappointment. They are afraid that if they come clean, they will be punished. This leads to secrecy or telling half-truths. Effective communication between the parent and the child forges an environment where things are discussed no matter how absurd their nature. Things are shared without judgment and sensible ways to right the wrong or prevent the same mistakes are advised. When kids feel heard and have their opinions valued, there is nothing left for them to hide. It relieves them to have someone who is there to listen and help them with their problems. Additionally, it boasts a child's confidence and self-esteem when they know they can rely on someone completely. They feel more empowered and backed by the connection they have with you.

Effective Ways to Improve Parent-Child Communication

Sadly, there aren't any parental manuals that teach parents what to do and what not to do. As each child is unique and beautiful in their own way, so is the style of raising them. There are up to six different types of parenting styles, which suggest that there is no universal method to guarantee to raise successful and happy kids. But since it all starts with how good or bad the communication between the child and the parent is, we first need to ensure that we are doing all in our power to strengthen our bond with them so that they can learn to trust us and rely on us to help them get past hardships and obstacles.

Be an Interested Parent

Who is a parent? Is he/she only a meal provider, a diaper-changer, or a sleeping cushion? No, a parent is much more than that. A parent listens to their child with genuine concern and curiosity. A parent, at times, goes overboard with emotions like standing to applaud for them when overwhelmed with their performance on stage. They are the listening ear kids need, the comfort they turn to when sick, tired, or scared.

Don't Argue Over "Who is Right"

To establish healthy communication where the child continues to look up to you for support, approval, and correction is pivotal. Often, parents, being more experienced and cultured, try to argue with children over who's right. Clearly, you must be but they are too naïve to see that. No one likes to be told that they are wrong, even when they are wrong. Turning every conversation into a fight about who's wrong and who's right, isn't going to help you. Instead, it will further distance you from your child and promote the habit of lying and secrecy. Keep your cool and listen attentively without judgment. Let them have their say and then, if asked, offer solutions and advice.

Include Them in Decision-Making

Another way to pave the way for healthy communication is by seeking their opinion over family matters that will affect them too. For instance, you and your partner may have decided to take a trip to Greece and you tell your kid that you are going to go there this summer. You thought they would be over the moon with the news, but they seem heartbroken. Upon inquiring, you find out that they wanted to go to Disneyland all this time and had been waiting to talk to you about it over the weekend. If they don't feel that their voice matters and opinions are valued, they will stop putting them forward.

Ask Them About Their Needs

Many kids aren't expressive when it comes to talking about their needs. They feel pushy and demanding and thus, find means to get things by themselves. As a parent, talk to them about their needs often. Maybe, what they need isn't something materialistic but rather help to solve a problem or advice to overcome hardship. Or maybe they just want to vent their frustration with someone to unburden themselves a little.

Avoid Imposing Ideas

If your child is opening up to you, it means that they genuinely feel that you can offer opinions and support. However, if you continue to impose your ideas over how they should do things instead of giving them the power to choose, it will drive them away. Parents who respond with close-minded opinions and act uptight do more harm than good. Instead of imposing things, try to have a dialogue with your children, where both of you share your ideas and opinions and then choose the one that seems the best. Moreover, stop trying to control them or problem-solve for them as it makes them feel trapped.

Chapter 7: Act like a Role Model - Period!

Nearly all of the habits our children pick up are the ones they see us embodying. Some are of course genetic like sleeping in the same pose as their father or making noises while chewing like their mother. However, all the other habits and behaviors are considered a skill which means that can be learned upon repetition. As a parent, you have to be extra careful about what behaviors your children are picking up from you when you are not noticing. They have been looking up to you for nearly everything since birth. In this chapter, we briefly go over the role of parents as ideal models for their kids and discuss the positive habits that will help parents raise transparent and honest kids.

Dear Parents, It all Starts with You

Youngsters mostly look up to or want to establish relationships with people older and wiser than themselves. They find mentors in their teachers, relatives, or parents. However, not everyone becomes a role model for them. They may love their parents but not consider them role models. They may be fascinated by someone for a different set of skills. For instance, if they are into the piano or violin, they may consider a professional player as their role model because they want to be just like them. An ideal role model must possess some desirable traits which are easy to follow and look up to. They must ignite passion and inspire motivation to change in the follower. They must help them thrive towards their goals and push them forward with their personal story, determination, or personality.

If you want to become your child's role model, here are the qualities you must demonstrate.

Role Models Have Good Morals and Values

Good values and morals rank the highest. Any role model must be able to inspire others with the work that they do and how they do it. Children only respect people who stay true to their words and practice what they preach. They are people who support the right causes and raise their voice against violence and rights violations. They are also honest and far from deceit.

Role Models Practice Acceptance

They don't disregard others or think of others beneath them. They have the drive to help others in their community and area of work. They want others to improve and be better human beings. They don't take pleasure in belittling someone. They are someone who, upon seeing someone in need, goes to their aid no matter what their circumstances or background is.

Role Models Overcome Obstacles Fearlessly

Unlike others, role models don't fear hardship but rather welcome it. They don't measure their success by where they are in their lives but rather by how many obstacles they have faced and overcome in their lives. Young people want to feel this empowered too. So this quality of braveness and commitment to not give up really speaks to them.

They are Creative and Optimistic

According to a youngster, a role model is someone that detests monotony. They have a positive outlook on life and are usually upbeat and happy. They are people who see the good in everything and the bright side of things even when situations are bad. They are always looking at creative means to improve their current state and do something that helps them and others in their surroundings.

They Have Clear-cut Values

Kids admire people who are able to live the life they visualize. They rely strongly on good and positive values. They never bend their morals to meet the requirements of someone else. They are always advocating for innovation and social change. The reason kids and teenagers admire thes traits is because someday they want to feel the same way and having someone like that in their life just makes the task seem less daunting.

Role Models Respect Others

Being respectful is another important trait of a role model. Not only do they value the people around them, but they also have respect for them. Like adults, kids want to feel respected too. They want their opinions to be valued and respected. They appreciate anyone that does so. According to them, role models should be selfless and hold non-prejudiced views.

4 Things Parents Who Raise Honest Kids do

Now that we have identified the mistakes and taken note of the things we do wrong, whether it is our timing or the way we are trying to communicate with our children, we now know what needs changing in order to raise honest kids. Remember when we were kids: we would spend hours playing with friends from the neighborhood, and there was always that one friend who was so chill about the scary ideas we sometimes had, like going to that empty house at the corner of the street or riding bikes without our hands on the handle? These were the sort of things we kept from our parents but not them. They would gloat about the activities of the day without fearing their reaction and response: their parents also seemed so interested and less judgmental than ours.

If you are still in touch with that friend, try to notice how different they are from you, who hid things from your parents, and lied about the days' activities. Notice the difference in the sort of relationship they have with everyone around them, especially their kids. Doesn't it feel like they have it all figured out and raising honest, confident, and independent kids?

The values and morals we model in ourselves are the ones our offspring take from us. It's like it rubs off them. This is why we must, at all times, be teaching them the habits that will help them improve their chances in the future, whether in terms of interpersonal relationships, career, or in life.

So, take a look at these four things that parents who raise honest kids have in them and try to embody the same in yourself.

They Model Honesty

Teaching kids the difference between right and wrong, good and bad, and acceptable and unacceptable behaviors and actions early on is an essential step to raising honest kids. Parents who understand this don't lie in front of their children. They speak the truth, even about the small things they could have easily lied about. For example, your mom came to pick you up from school while your dad waited at home. Your mother notices a friend of hers on the sidewalk and stops to have a chat. When you guys return and your father asks what took you so long, your mother doesn't answer with lies like 'getting stuck in traffic' but rather speaks the truth.

They Accept Their Mistakes

We are all humans and thus, prone to making mistakes. Parents make mistakes too but rather than hiding them, they accept them to teach their children that this is what they should do too. Owning up to one's mistakes takes courage. Seeing their parents own up to their mistakes without guilt or shame teaches c children to do the same too.

They're Authoritative

They are controlling but not dictators. They allow their kids to make mistakes so that they can learn valuable lessons about honesty and the dangers of secrecy that can only be learned with experience. They don't punish their children because they know that only promotes a culture of secrecy and lying. Instead, they discipline them in a calm manner. That doesn't mean there are no consequences for the way they behave, it is just that they aren't harsh or brutal.

They Wait before Judging

No one has ever learned a new skill in a day. If we want to learn a new language, it takes classes and extensive coaching to be able to speak it fluently. It's the same with habits. The more we practice them, the better we get at them. This is what parents try to raise honest kids to understand. They know that learning to speak the truth and not keep secrets takes time. Children need to feel confident that they can go to their parents and discuss anything and everything. They need to first develop an understanding with their parents, and the parents needs to allow them as much time as they need. They don't rush them to act well-mannered in a day and lose all bad habits. They allow their children to gradually make the transition on their own terms.

Chapter 8: Raising an Honest Child

Raising an honest child is hard. There will be times you will find yourself lying to their face about something the minute you are teaching them not to lie. Not to mention, they will be least bothered by the upcoming lecture because one, according to them they don't lie and two, they are still going to at least continue with the hiding part because that is an essential part of growth.

So that leaves you with fewer chances of success, especially if they are already in their teens and looking at you as a potential enemy, someone rather uptight and backward.

However, if you approach the topic in ways that don't come off as lecturing but rather healthy discussions in the form of storytelling, you may increase your chances of getting them thinking. This will be the first step towards victory.

In this final chapter of the book, we will list ways that will help you get your voice heard loud and clear. Practice these and later pat yourself on the back for having raised an honest child.

Responding to Lies – Strategies to Help Parents Improve Transparency

Honesty a habit that never loses its charm and continues to add to one's respect and reputation. So how do we raise honest children, you ask? Here's how:

Model Honesty

This goes without saying and seems rather obvious too, but kids observe and they imitate. If you aren't being the perfect flag-bearer for honesty, they aren't going to hear a word of it. If you lie to your kids, whether it is for their safety or out of worry, they will see it as a means to get away with things. When kids see their parents preaching about honesty on one hand and telling lies on the other, it sends them mixed signals which they are too young to comprehend. If they are too young to make the distinction between safe and unsafe, and acceptable and unacceptable lies, they will have a hard time listening to you and modeling honesty within themselves.

Don't Provide Them with Opportunities to Lie

Don't invite lying. One way parents bring it onto themselves is by providing the child with opportunities to lie as a way of testing them. If you notice they have spilled a glass of juice on their shirts or used your lipstick, don't ask them who did it or how it happened. 99% of the time, after being caught red-handed, children are going to lie and blame someone else. You already know who did what, so instead of offering them a chance to lie, simply say, "Looks like you have spilled some juice, let's go clean it up and be careful the next time" or "I see you have used mommy's lipsticks without her permission. Let's get you cleaned up and please ask permission to use it next time."

Notice how these sentences eliminate or lessen the burden of blame and make the conversation less confrontational? Chances are, if they paid attention and realized that not every mistake is rewarded with punishment and shame, they will try to come to clean next time.

Teach Them to Say the Hard Truths

Sometimes, it is more important to uphold morals than to care about someone getting hurt. For example, your son's friend has a habit of stealing things whenever they visit your house. Your son might have known and kept a secret, assuming you won't find out. However, as a responsible parent, it is your job to encourage your son to do the right thing and tell his friend to stop stealing. Of course, the friend will deny any attempt at stealing first and will have their feelings hurt, but it will also set them on the right path if they choose to quit.

Stop Rewarding Lies

When a child lies, there is usually something motivating them. There is a reason why they decide to hide the truth, and if you reward them with what they are seeking, they begin to see it as an effective strategy. Stop giving them what they need until they tell you why they need it. Don't reward their every wish and demand without realizing that it will eventually spoil them and make them feel privileged.

Praise Them When Honest

On the other hand, if you do want to reward them, reward them when you see them telling the truth. Catch them telling the truth, act elated that they did, and reward this behavior with an ice-cream treat or more time watching TV. The point is, when they notice a certain behavior leads to a prize, they will try to model more of it – just for the sake of the reward.

Keep Promises

If they keep finding you breaking your promises to them, they will do the same. Thus, it is again down to becoming the role model they would want to follow. Keep promises to ensure the trust between you and your children isn't broken.

Be Calm While Disciplining

A lot of times, we respond to a lying act rather harshly. We yell and punish the child for lying and take away their gadgets, or ground them at home. In households where punishments are doled out harshly, kids learn to lie earlier. This doesn't mean there isn't any need to discipline them, but rather it means it's best to impart discipline in a calm and composed manner. If they have been caught lying or have come to you to tell the truth, don't have an emotional reaction. Simply state the facts as to why they shouldn't have lied and should try not to, moving forward.

Mess Up Some Facts

One of the most fun ways of teaching them about honesty is by messing up some common facts in the stories or poems they love. For example, Mary had a little 'cat' instead of a 'lamb'. Let them point out the messed up fact. You can also make false statements like you are wearing a red-colored shirt when in reality, it is yellow. When children feel challenged in such a manner, they learn about the impact of a lie and how it can change the whole story.

Set Clear Expectations

Another important thing parents must do is be clear about what is expected of them. They must know the rules they must abide by to avoid disappointment and lying. Kids tend to lie when the expectations are either too high or hazy and they don't end up living up to them. So to avoid embarrassment and shaming, they lie to get away.

Give Them Privacy

It doesn't matter how young or old they are, privacy and space is an essential thing to offer your children. Being overprotective or adopting a 'helicopter parenting' style would only make them feel suffocated, which will lead them to start making excuses and tell lies to get you off their back. Don't be too intrusive and wait for them to come to you if something is bothering them.

Share Positive Stories

If they are still young, it is the best time to read stories about characters who lied but came clean about their mistake or wrongdoing to their parents. According to a research study led by psychologist Kang Lee at the University of Toronto, children aged three to seven are more likely to be inspired by positive stories than negative ones. This means that stories that end up scaring them at the end like the *Boy who Cried Wolf* aren't going to be as impactful as *George Washington and the Cherry Tree*.

Make Promise to Them

If you are curious about something they did or something that happened to them, before asking them to tell you all about it, ask them to promise you first that they will answer only with the truth when you ask a question. This increases the likelihood of them speaking the truth. However, this should be used rarely, or else it will lose its efficacy.

Conclusion

Being a parent, in its essence, is a demanding role. Even though we sign up for it willingly and cheerfully, we mustn't forget the challenges it brings along with it. As your baby grows into a toddler, child, adolescent, and into a teenager, their needs grow too. They no longer rely on you for feeds, sleep, and cleaning only. To make a respectable place for themselves in the world out there, they also need good morals, ethics, and values to live by.

Teaching them to be honest and respectable are the core values we instill in them and yet, despite our best efforts, we often catch them lying straight to our faces with confident-eyes and a calm tone. So where are we doing wrong? Why do they still turn to lie, deceit, and secrecy when we teach them not to? This is rather complicated and also the goal of the book. Not only did we want to give parents the answer to this, but we also wanted them to explore with us the many things that they are doing wrong. Things, like being dishonest themselves, keeping secrets, and teaching their children to keep secrets for them, are few of the mistakes we make.

But there is a light at the end of the tunnel. We now have the means to prevent secrecy and model honesty in our children using tools like open and supportive communication, becoming an ideal role model to them, and teaching them about the dangers of secrecy and lying.

With continued work, the right values will make a home in their hearts and help you, as a parent, to take some pressure off your shoulders. Once they learn of the many advantages being honest and transparent has, they will, themselves, choose to respect others and value their feelings.

References

5 Types of Liars and How to Spot Them. (2019, October 8). https://www.womenworking.com/5-types-of-liars-and-how-to-spot-them/

Francis, L. (2020, February 26). Honest Kids Come From Parents Who Do These 5 Things. https://www.fatherly.com/parenting/parents-honest-kids-5-things/

Feldman, R. (2002, June 10). UMass researcher finds most people lie in everyday conversation. Hampshire County, Massachusetts, United States.

Heid, M. (n.d.). Your Brain On: Lying. https://www.shape.com/lifestyle/mind-and-body/your-brain-lying

Honesty Really Is Healthy. (2012, August 8). https://www.huffpost.com/entry/honesty-healthy-lies-truth_n_1748144

How to Prevent Kids from Keeping Secrets. (n.d.). https://www.indiaparenting.com/raising-children/130_5389/how-to-prevent-kids-from-keeping-secrets.html

It's A Thin Between Privacy & Secrecy. (2018, February 5). https://couplesacademy.org/2018/02/05/its-a-thin-between-privacy-secrecy/

Kelly, A. E. (2012, August 4). Lying Less Linked to Better Health, New Research Finds. Orlando, Florida, United States of America.

Levine, E. E., & Cohen, T. R. (2018). You can handle the truth: Mispredicting the consequences of honest communication. Journal of Experimental Psychology: General, 1400–1429.

Ni, P. (2015, July 22). 7 Key Signs of a Lying Child or Teenager. https://www.psychologytoday.com/us/blog/communication-success/201507/7-key-signs-lying-child-or-teenager

Pssst...Why Is My Teen Keeping Secrets From Me? (2011, July 31). https://www.psychologytoday.com/us/blog/youth-and-tell/201107/pssstwhy-is-my-teen-keeping-secrets-me

Smith, C. E., & Rizzo, M. T. (2017). Children's confession- and lying-related emotion expectancies: Developmental differences and connections to parent-reported confession behavior. Journal of Experimental Child Psychology, 113-128.

Smith, J. A. (n.d.). What's Good about Lying? https://greatergood.berkeley.edu/article/item/whats_good_about_lying

The Secret Lives of Teens They Don't Want You to Know About. (2019, May 20). https://www.allprodad.com/the-secret-lives-of-teens-they-dont-want-you-to-know-about/

Why Honesty Is Good for Our Kids' Health. (2020, April 20). https://www.parent.com/honesty-good-kids-health/

Verschuere, B., Spruyt, A., Meijer, E. H., & Otgaar, H. (2010). The ease of lying. Consciousness and Cognition, 908-11.

HOW PARENTS CAN FOSTER FRIENDSHIP IN CHILDREN

Begin a Meaningful Relationship With Your Child as Both Parent and Friend - Without the Power Struggle

FRANK DIXON

© **Copyright 2020 - All rights reserved.**

The content contained within this book may not be reproduced, duplicated or transmitted without direct written permission from the author or the publisher.

Under no circumstances will any blame or legal responsibility be held against the publisher, or author, for any damages, reparation, or monetary loss due to the information contained within this book, either directly or indirectly.

Legal Notice:

This book is copyright protected. It is only for personal use. You cannot amend, distribute, sell, use, quote or paraphrase any part, or the content within this book, without the consent of the author or publisher.

Disclaimer Notice:

Please note the information contained within this document is for educational and entertainment purposes only. All effort has been executed to present accurate, up to date, reliable, complete information. No warranties of any kind are declared or implied. Readers acknowledge that the author is not engaged in the rendering of legal, financial, medical or professional advice. The content within this book has been derived from various sources. Please consult a licensed professional before attempting any techniques outlined in this book.

By reading this document, the reader agrees that under no circumstances is the author responsible for any losses, direct or indirect, that are incurred as a result of the use of the information contained within this document, including, but not limited to, errors, omissions, or inaccuracies.

Introduction

Good friendships in life are a godsend. No matter what age you are, you'll never forget the time spent with friends. The thought takes us back to those carefree days and nights when we used to play outside or share stories in secret under a blanket. The joy they bring into our lives and the colors they add to our palette is truly remarkable.

There are many benefits to early childhood friendships. For many children, their social circles allow them an outlet for their curious mind, beyond the home or classroom. Children learn and grow from each other, much like lion cubs at play. Friendships also help us set and accomplish our goals, whether to complete a project or find extracurriculars. It's always easier for a child to join a sports team if they join with a friend. Friends encourage us and boost our confidence. Looking back, we all know how much easier it was to be social when we had a buddy system.

Equally important, a good friend is always there to pick us up when we fall. A real connection to someone can feel like a port in a storm. With the rapid changes in any child's life, including the significant shift of puberty, a social circle becomes important to make sense of it all. These ideas even have sound academic backing, as studies have shown that friendships help children develop many emotional and social skills, and improve their sense of belonging (Jones et al., 2015).

A child behavior expert, Paul Schwartz, suggests that friendships contribute to the development of skills such as sensitivity towards one another and acceptance of differences in opinions (Schwartz, n.d.). A social circle also enables children to keep pace with age-appropriate behaviors. According to Schwartz, children with smaller circles reported early trouble interacting with peers and depicting emotional stability.

In another research study, scientists also found that friendships can have a positive impact on the academic performances of children (Fletcher et al., 2013). Friends help each other in discouraging deviant behavior, especially those within the same academic program, and often report high self-esteem and advanced coping mechanisms.

In this book, we will explore the importance of long-lasting friendships and help our children form them without hesitation. We will also look at the important relationship between a parent and child, and whether we need to seek "friendship" with our children.

Chapter 1: Understanding Friendship

Author C.S. Lewis (*The Chronicles of Narnia*) once said, "Friendship is born at that moment when one person says to another: "What! You too? I thought I was the only one" (1960). This idea has reflections even in antiquity, as Greek philosopher Plato also spoke on this unique relationship, stating, "Similarity begets friendship" (2013). I think we can all agree that similar interests are often an indicator of close friendships. But that's not always entirely true. How many of us had or still have friends that are complete opposites of ourselves? If we like romantic comedies, they would insist on science fiction. If we want chocolate, they would prefer vanilla. Our interests may not align, but we still consider them good friends.

These relationships are so important to us, so intriguing, that researchers throughout history have always wanted to know how they develop. Was there some hidden motive behind friendship? Were these relationships based on a tit-for-tat, or, "you scratch my back and I scratch yours" approach? Or was there something more abstract to it all?

To solve this puzzle, researchers looked at the animal kingdom for a clue. Animals were believed to have less manipulation in their behaviors, or less ulterior motives - unlike human beings - and thought to be motivated simply by food or mates (Mourier et al., 2012).

In one study, a group of French scientists observed 133 blacktip reef sharks in an attempt to determine if they occupied the same space at the same time, and if they had similar groupings to humans (Mourier et al., 2012). After monitoring their behavior for weeks, these scientists were surprised to note that many sharks indeed preferred the company of specific others and even went out of their way to avoid the rest. These groupings could be considered parallel to human social circles.

In another experiment, researchers asked participants to form a list of ten of their closest friends, and to assign one hundred "points" between them on a scale of closeness (DeScioli & Kurzban, 2009). When one group of participants were told that their answers would be kept confidential, they rated their friends truthfully. However, when another group was told that their results would become public, those participants allocated their points equally among their friends. In the latter group, each friend received around ten points, while in the former, some had gotten twenty while others had just five. The study concluded that friendship heavily affects one's reputation. Humans want to maintain a good reputation among friends, in order to stay connected.

The Meaning of Friendship

While scientists continue to study the factors of friendship, we can run some general conclusions. Friendship is built on trust, intimacy, and esteem between two or more people. It suggests a sense of safety and confidentiality, and acts as a support system. What separates friendship from basic companions or acquaintances are five items:

1. *Interaction.* Friendship is regarded at its core as a dyadic relationship - occurring between two people - and is based on interactions between those people. Those interactions build history, familiarity, and expectations. Meeting those expectations builds trust. Styles of interaction have evolved over the years, but online interactions still develop the familiarity essential to friendship.

2. *Reciprocated Affection.* Friendship is a give-and-take relationship, where both partners are invested in the lives of each other. A unique bond is created through their mutual attraction and respect.

3. *No Legalities.* Unlike other legal relationships, friendship isn't obligatory or legally binding. There is no contract to sign, but simply based on mutual consent. Thus, these bonds can become as strong or as weak as your level of investment.

4. *Egalitarian in Nature*. Both individuals share the same power and voice as the other. Friendship is democratic. It is thus difficult to maintain friendship between individuals with different power levels - especially if they share a home or work environment.

5. *Shared activities*. Participating in a project or experience together builds companionship. Companionship is a primary foundation of any blooming friendship. It develops when people feel comfortable and valued in each other's company.

These five features are what differentiate friendships from other common relationships. The presence of any, if not all, of these features differentiates a friend from another peer group.

What Connects Us?

It may be shared interests, or it may be a sense of security, but what else can bring us together?

A common feature of friendship and social circles is shared histories. This could mean shared experiences or familiar stories through race, geography, ethnicity, or religion. In this case, a similar background may develop similar understandings and perspectives of the world. Shared histories could also mean some similar experience two individuals have gone through, such as the separation or loss of a parent. It is much easier to talk to someone with the same experiences as you, especially on a difficult or unfamiliar subject.

Two individuals could also share common values. Common values create friendships with less strain, while differing views have an extra stress factor. However, again, differences don't mean the relationship won't work, and in many ways, differences can actually create a valuable learning experience. That shared experience then further strengthens a bond.

Importantly, friendships also tend to develop along lines of equality. There must be equality between both partners for a friendship to succeed in the long-term. If one individual feels that they give without receiving the same compassion and care in return, they may feel slighted, or taken for granted. Both partners need support and encouragement to create value in the relationship. Thus, both partners need to put in equal effort.

The Qualities of a Good Friend

The general qualities of a good friend are familiar to us. They share unique interests and skills. They have a unique personality that blends with ours. We always feel comfortable in their company. But unfortunately, there isn't an exact formula to determine who your friends will be.

We connect with who we communicate with. It can be a neighbor, a classmate, or another family with a similar commute. You could meet in the grocery store, or at the playground. Introductions have no set format. If children are younger, their interactions are more natural, with less learned social anxiety to hold them back. They sit with, learn with, and play with others in an unseeming pattern. Eventually, familiarity forms and bonds are created. For older children, interactions are based on shared experiences and common interests. They may have a project together in art class, or play the same instrument in the school band.

Teenagers are much more complex. At this age, new social dynamics emerge, social pressures offer new expectations, and puberty sends emotions into overdrive. In this overwhelming stage, friends are very important to help navigate these new feelings. They are formed through common experiences, but grasped quickly, and held on to tightly. In this way, it can be difficult for a student in a new school to make friends, as friendships and cliques have been pre-established. But once a real connection is made, it can mean the world to that new student.

In all, the following traits are considered the most admired qualities of a good friend:

1. *Trustworthiness*. Trust is what keeps a relationship bound. When a friend is trustworthy, it means that you can be your true self with them, acting without

pretense. You can rely on them to share private experiences, acknowledge feelings, and keep a secret without judgement. True and trustworthy friends offer us a safe space.

2. *Kindness.* A kind friend is considerate and compassionate. They stand with you, comfort you, and help you without expecting anything in return. They are genuinely interested in your life and want you to have the best.

3. *Honesty.* An honest friend doesn't offer fake appreciation. They are straightforward when they need to be, and will tell you when they are confused or disappointed by a choice you make. But they will also gladly tell you when they love and respect your choices. They are invested in your wellbeing.

4. *Unconditional Support.* A genuine friend will support you in a mistake and help you grow from it. Their support may come in different forms, such as emotional support when we feel low or insecure, or practical support when we need to handle a problem. They will always have your back.

5. *Acceptance.* We all carry flaws and imperfections. A true friend will accept those of us, without trying to mold us

into someone else. Without envy or condescension, an accepting friend will let you exist as you are.

6. *Emotional Availability.* We should all be able to feel wanted, heard, and seen. An available friend knows how to pull us out of our miseries and look at the bright side. They pop over when we feel lonely, and don't leave until they've boosted our mood. Always just a call or text away.

7. *Comfort.* A friend should make us feel safe, protected, and covered. When we are close friends with someone, there is no reluctance when it comes to asking for favors. With a close friend, it doesn't feel like putting your partner in a bad position. We trust that they really need the favor, and they trust us to take care of it. Every bond strengthens when ideas are heard and accepted.

8. *Forgiveness.* A forgiving friend will not press you if you fall short in your responsibilities. They don't hold grudges, they listen to reason, and they are willing to sort things out. They trust you to learn and give you space to grow

Chapter 2: Essential Friendship Building Skills

As friendship is such an important part of our lives, contributing in part to our very personalities, how do we, as parents of toddlers and adolescents, help our children make friends? It can be difficult to accept that our role is limited. Ultimately, a child needs to make these decisions on their own, and so the best a parent can do is teach them the right skills. Many of these skills are straightforward, focusing on kindness, proper conversation, inclusion, and active listening. Those skills are helpful because they make those first few interactions less stressful. That old adage rings true - first impressions are hard to break. It will always be harder later to nudge in and join a conversation that has already started. To establish friendships, social skills are important, helping to make introductions more natural and less forced. With these skills in their pocket, your child will be best prepared for a future of friendship.

Building Blocks of an Everlasting Friendship

Social skills include interpersonal skills, such as active listening, cooperation, collaborative play, patience, and empathy. These are important to teach early on as they set the pace for improved relationships over a lifetime. Children who develop emotional intelligence, kindness, generosity, and empathy are likely to do well in academics and lead happier lives than those who lack these essential skills. Happier lives mean success, reduced stress, and fulfilled goals. As parents we need to do our best to encourage our children to form strong bonds and have someone to share ideas and thoughts with. Once these connections are made they create an intertwined growth - stronger together than apart.

Communication Skills

Friendship, and any other relationship, relies on communication. Friendship is very difficult to sustain between friends without talking to each other. Without similar interests or values, friends may find it difficult to share with one another, and drift apart. At times, conflicting values can stimulate good conversation between friends, but those conversations require careful attention and balance. Therefore, good communication skills are essential for every child. They must know how to start, carry on, and end a conversation when appropriate. They must develop a delicate social filter to speak openly, but carefully, to make others feel interested, but not uncomfortable. They must also be willing to share when the conversation requires it, and listen in turn.

Listening Skills

Listening skills are the hidden star of good conversation. It is not enough to have something to say, but rather, to have the right thing to say. It is not talking for the sake of filling a silence. From an early age, children are naturally excellent listeners, soaking up the world around them and reacting with deep empathy. As they are socialized into conversation, they tend to lose this skill as they try to make an impact on their environments. Parents, in turn, need to reinforce these active listening skills with their developing children. An active listener is one who doesn't just react, but responds empathetically. Teach your children to focus not just on the verbal cues, but also on non-verbal cues like a friend's body language, facial expressions, and tone of voice. Focus on what is being said without distractions, or getting lost in their thoughts. And importantly, they must read these cues for the right time to respond. For example, when the moment requires it, or their partner has said their piece. Often, a friend just needs to let it out and be heard. Try not to offer unsolicited advice or try to fix things unless asked to.

Fair Play Skills

Younger children, in particular, have a hard time sharing and following fair play. Playing is really only fun when both players are fair. Rules need to be softly reinforced to dissuade cheating. A bad experience at playtime does not lend itself to a lasting bond of friendship. Naturally, there will be some drama in encouraging balanced play time, but better the drama be on you as a disciplinarian, than more personal and amongst the children themselves. Eventually, they will learn to expect to share, and the drama will subside.

Empathy

We all must be considerate of the feelings of others. But as a less tangible skill, this can be difficult to teach. Simply encourage your children to look for and recognize the feelings of others. Don't disregard them as if they aren't important. Treat other individuals like icebergs and look for the other 90% hidden below the surface. Body language lends context to conversation, so seek out these clues. Your child is a natural empath when it's born, feeding on the emotions of the mother and father. So feed these empathy abilities and let them blossom - don't stifle them so soon in the difficulties of a daily schedule. Trust in yourself and be patient. If done correctly, your child should come to accept the feelings of others, without judgment. Again, that feeling of being seen and heard can be an incredibly powerful tool to create lasting friendships.

Patience

We all need to practice this skill, not just children. So do your best as you teach your child, and be patient even with yourself. This skill applies across any context, whether in conversation or at play. Give others a chance when they are speaking, without interrupting. Look out for others, and understand that we will all have a turn when the moment is right.

Accepting Wins and Losses

Life isn't fair and games certainly aren't either. Someone has to lose in order for someone to win.

Whether your child wins or loses, they should know how to accept it graciously. It is difficult to stay friends with an ungracious loser or a gloating winner. The same rules of fair play apply here. Teach your children to express decently and with grace. Encourage them to win or lose without excuses or grudges. Games are practice for real world encounters, so be sure to play them respectfully.

Acceptance Skills

Children must be taught to accept others as they are. They shouldn't discriminate against someone based on their height, weight, or other physical features. They shouldn't belittle others from a different background or experience. They mustn't bully or fight with people who don't share the same opinions as them. They should instead appreciate and accept everyone's unique qualities and differences. In doing so, the doors of friendship open more frequently.

Conflict Resolution

In any relationship, conflicts, arguments, and differences of opinions are bound to occur. Your child may insist on playing a certain game indoors while their friend wishes to ride bikes outside in the sun. As friends, they must be able to compromise, whichever form it takes to them. Encourage your children not to frame conflicts as win-or-lose encounters. There will always be a third, fourth, or fifth option. Real friends will look for these other options. Empathy is a great skill here, so that we can see from our friend's perspective. Teach them to put aside their personal gains and find ways in which they can gain together as partners.

Does My Parenting Style Impact My Child's Friendships?

As parents, we want our kids to have the right friends. People who lift them, inspire them, and motivate them to pursue their goals in life. We might want to help them first and be there for them before others, but as children grow older, they stop relying on us and rely more on their friends. It can be a painful truth that friends may understand each other better than a parent-child relationship can. The unconditional love of a parent is strongest above all, but it can also be healthy for a child to have multiple support systems.

We often assume that parenting is hard. However, we occasionally forget how hard it can be for a child too. They go through a lot, and very quickly. It takes real commitment to stay friends with someone. Having someone to hang out with at school, in college, or at the office is encouraging. But everyone is raised in a different household, and under a different parenting style. Children emerge from our homes, each uniquely affected by that parenting style, and use our past-down knowledge to build their friendships. Interestingly, new research suggests that parents can be one of the many reasons why some kids struggle with making friends at school or in college.

Published in Science Daily, a recent joint study from the University of Jyvaskyla and Florida Atlantic University suggested that negative parenting strategies, which lower a child's self-esteem, ultimately affects the formation of friendships in their lives (Dickson et al., 2018). Collecting data from 1,523 children in grades one to six, the study analyzed the characteristics of the parents and their parenting style, as well as the friendships of their children. The collaborative team from both universities identified three important elements of parenting when it comes to forming relationships:

1. The degree to which warmth and affection was shown to the child
2. Behavioral control (using strict rules and regulations)
3. Psychological control (using guilt and shaming to impact behavior)

The researchers further suggested that children from households where parents exerted psychological control were most likely to have friendships dissolve later in life. Those children reported less trust, poor self-esteem, and a lack of social skills; including poor communication and confidence in their abilities to form strong relationships.

As parents, if we fail to teach the basic skills of friendship, and instead become highly demanding and unappreciative parents, we can directly impact the development of our children's relationships.

Chapter 3: How to Make Friends

As a parent, there is much we can do to help our kids establish long-term friendships. We encourage them to say hi to someone new, or to share a toy when they are young. We play a key role in helping them make those first impressions. However, friendship looks quite different when kids grow older. Parents play a smaller role in their child's social life as they develop a mind of their own and a drive for self-determination. Guidance and monitoring are, however, still the duties of every parent. Just because they have brought someone home from school one day, doesn't mean that they are the best choice for your child. As we discussed in chapter one, not everyone carries the best qualities of friendship, or has your child's goodwill in mind.

In this chapter, we will discuss the role played by parents in fostering friendships at different ages.

Befriending at Different Ages

To help keep our children safe, we need to cultivate good, inspiring, and trustworthy friends around them. The last thing you want is for your child to have their heart broken by a friend who didn't respect them. Not only that, but it is also our job to ensure that the activities among friends are age-appropriate and safe. Negative influences surround us, and a child needs to learn critical awareness and media literacy to successfully navigate their environment. That teaching role still falls upon the parents. It will always be awkward to have "The Talk", but the parent is the most important resource for a child, and needs to offer that lifeline - even if the child doesn't accept it at first. Let your children know you are always ready to talk if they are, but don't push them. Open communication and active listening skills are skills that can help parents too. It allows them to stay involved in their child's life, without lying or secrecy on either end.

So remember to consider your options carefully, and while you can't always select the friends for your child - you can certainly push them in the right direction.

Young Friendships

Kindergarten friends are often made by instinct. For instance, they may want to sit with someone special, or share their toys only with another. As parents, your role here is to be present to ensure they do so safely. You will want to display positive play relationships, and responsible behaviors. For parents, it helps to notice the strengths and weaknesses of their kid, and encourage growth in both areas - but give them space to develop. If you have a particularly shy kid, you can always pop in to check that they feel comfortable, but let them discover their own limits.

Young children are especially great empaths, so use this opportunity to have them check in with their emotions. Help them safely experience hurt, pain, or sadness - and what each means. Help them discover these emotions as displayed by others. Develop their empathy to encourage these skills later in life. Talk to them about keeping calm and not getting frustrated.

School-Age Friendships

School-going years are a fertile time to build friendships. School friends often become life-long friends, and those long-term friends offer a unique perspective to keep you in check as you grow and change. But children are choosier in school. They need time to find similar interests and see if the other can be trusted with their secrets or not. New responsibilities have also entered the child's life. This is a great opportunity to connect with others by sharing those responsibilities, such as studying together for a test. They are also meeting more types of people than ever before, and discovering more about themselves.

As a parent, your role from this point on is that of a coach more than a playmate. You are still in charge, but relegated to the sidelines. But you also provide more direction than ever as they face their intimidating new world. Therefore, continue to emphasize and build their social skills. If your child is shy, teach them coping strategies for peer conflict. If your child is temperamental, teach alternate expressions than anger. Above all, encourage taking a moment to slow down and give others a chance to be their friend, without letting negative thinking overpower them. After all, every other child is in the same place - they're nervous and want to make friends too!

When your child brings a friend home, be welcoming. Go through the rules in the house quickly before leaving them to enjoy themselves. Your child should be a good host in their own home, as well as a good guest in another's. Talk to them about being respectful and asking permission. Teach them to be polite, humble, and accepting.

Get involved one way or the other in your child's life when they are at school. This will allow you to keep an eye on them, but more importantly, provide you with context to their life. For instance, you can join a club event, volunteer to help with fundraising, or join a school sports club. But know your boundaries and don't embarrass anyone. If you notice that they aren't happy about the involvement and look for ways to avoid meeting you when you visit their school, take a step back and don't push them. Be present but tone down the visits.

If the thought of your children having access to a phone scares you, then delay giving them one, and explain to them why. Develop the necessary social literacy skills before you give in. But always remember that a significant amount of communication and bonding takes place online, and this too can be a good opportunity to develop friendships - if done safely and carefully. If you aren't sure about the usage, it is best to put it off until necessary. Consider also making a rule to not have a pin code, but don't snoop without permission - this could severely damage any relationship - especially a parent-child relationship.

Eventually, your child may find a best friend. They will do everything together, and they will become inseparable. As a parent, the first thing to do is get to know the family of your child's friend. This will make the relationship smoother, as both the parents will be encouraging the strong bond that has been, or is in the process of forming. Be sure to check in with your child frequently to see how they feel about the relationship. These feelings can be intense, and if bent out of shape, can be damaging to emotional growth.

Use this as an opportunity to continue discussions of empathy and the importance of healthy communication. Advise them on the many emotions they are going to experience when things get patchy or rough between them and their friend. Encourage them to see the bigger picture for any change in a friends' behavior, before they accuse them of being a bad friend. If there is trouble, and it is safe, encourage them to stick with their friend - they could probably use someone to talk to. This is the moment when listening skills come in handy.

Teenage Friendships

This is the most difficult phase to navigate for both parents and their kids. They are going through so many hormonal transitions, and academics have become increasingly more important - ramping up the pressure even further. It can take a toll on their mental and emotional health. Sadly, this is also the age when distance between parents and children grows wider. Children will inevitably push back against the involvement of parents in their lives. They prefer privacy and are rather choosy about what they share with their parents. At this moment of your own evolving relationship with your child, it can be a difficult time to fully help them develop their other relationships. But be patient with yourself and stick with it - there is light around the corner.

At this age, negative influences start to enter your child's life. Drugs, parties, and sexual experimentation will be considered, but not necessarily experienced. This is the moment where trust between a parent and child needs to be stronger than ever. Instead of dwelling on the bad, try to focus on the good. If you dwell on the negative possibilities, you will create nothing but stress for yourself and your child. Inculcate them with positive experiences. Ensure that their health is your number one priority. Ensure that they are taking care of themselves and their hygiene. Talk to them about the importance of being safe. Teach them about responsibility and how losing control can impact their future. Sit them down and have a chat about intercourse and how to navigate with precaution. But then do your very best to take a step back and let them discover for themselves. Be their safety net, but don't hover and make them want to escape you. If you've taught them to the best of your ability, and shared all the information you have, they should be okay. You turned out okay after all, didn't you? Have some faith in them, and in yourself.

Give them space, but don't leave them hanging. Their body is changing and their moods are swinging wildly with new hormones and social pressures. Talk to them about these changes so they understand them. In fact, this would be a great moment to encourage them to talk to their friends, who are probably experiencing the same things. Allow the friends to be each other's support system, and take a small step back.

As kids are at the brink of becoming teenagers, their preferences may change in a week. For instance, someone who loved to play with dolls may one day want to throw them all away. Someone who loved to read books might be interested in some game time. All these moments will affect your child too. But when preferences change, so do friendships. Maybe the reason your child and their best friend hung out all the time was that they loved to gossip and do things together. But what if a boyfriend/girlfriend has taken their place? They are bound to feel lonely and taken for granted. So help them see through this and be a rock for them in this moment. Help them navigate their feelings as only a parent can.

Teach them to stand up for themselves if they feel they are being taken advantage of by anybody. They shouldn't have to feel neglected or make up for someone else's shortcomings. Some relationships are not worth keeping or fighting for. Both sides need to be invested. Encourage them to talk it out with a friend or former friend to resolve amicably. Strangely, sometimes you have to walk away in order to be someone's best friend in the moment.

Chapter 4: Friendships in School

School-age children need friends for healthy mental and emotional development. Be it heartbreaks or laughter during the time spent together, they learn many social skills just by being together. Kids who are unable to learn these skills at a young age will face difficulty later in life as they try to adapt. Friendship is more than just having a partner in crime, or a playmate. Friendship teaches children how to communicate better, to resolve conflicts, and to cooperate.

As they work and play together, young children become more able to control their emotions and express them with precision. They also learn to take note of the emotions of others and feel what they are feeling. Friendship also teaches them good negotiation skills, as well as how to cope with challenges. It improves their overall perspective about life because they feel looked after and valued. This also improves their attitude and the way they approach opportunities. Good friends even inspire their counterparts to do better in school. They can help each other problem-solve, study together, and healthily discuss things.

A healthy friendship also improves our self-esteem by providing support to think outside of the box and to give our best shot at everything. Teenagers especially can benefit from a support network of friends. Having one or more trustworthy and uplifting friends can help form a network to pull everyone through health issues like depression, anxiety, eating disorders, and lack of confidence - all by working together.

However, you shouldn't expect a drama-free transition into teenage years and a teenage network of friends. As any child enters their teen years, the drama will be unavoidable as anxiety brings emotions to the forefront. There will be confusion, sexual partners, and priorities changing. When that happens, it is also a parent's role to help them navigate their way through those changes. But most importantly, parents need to know how to get involved - without being too involved!

How to Help My Child Navigate Friendship Issues

So Natalie told Chrissy what I specifically told her not to. I kept her secret about that incident in the bathroom last week. Then why did she have to humiliate me like that in front of the whole science lab?

Sound familiar? If not - it may soon. Despite all your best intentions, and every effort to teach good communication skills, teenagers will eventually learn to speak rather abstractly and obscure the details. They may get offended over what seem to you like little things, but to them are the most important things in the world. And you need to be able to accept this when the time comes. Often the little things are small representations of a much larger problem, so don't brush them away so easily. Patience is key, just trust that your child will open up to you, their trusted source, when they are ready.

Sometimes, it isn't your child causing the scene but rather mutual friends, leaving your child confused and alone. If there are three best friends and two of them decide to have a fight and not talk to one another, the third friend gets punished in that contract for no reason. They may even be pressured into taking a side, and feel they have to prove their friendship to both others individually.

Social drama is common among adolescents. As a parent, if you notice that it is affecting the mental health of your child, you should be concerned. Sometimes, without you realizing, your child may be in a bullied position, simply for trying to prove their loyalty to another.

Therefore, to understand the role you have to play in all this, we have prepared a list of Do's and Don'ts:

Do

1. *Lend Your Ear.* The first thing you need to do to help your child navigate through social drama is to listen. If they come to you with a problem, hear them attentively and ask them if they would like to discuss the possible solutions or

just vent. Pay attention to their non-verbal cues and reciprocate the same to let them know you understand them.

2. *Probe.* As soon as they are done talking, ask them open-ended questions about how they think you can help them. Ask them about their opinions, views, and feelings on the event to know what they went through.

3. *Show Empathy.* Empathizing with them is another way to create that safe space for your child to be more expressive. When they sense that you are genuinely concerned and eager to help, they will feel much better.

4. *Brainstorm Solutions Together.* Now that you two are on the same page, the next sensible step is to work together as partners to look for possible solutions. Even if you know what they should do, don't enforce it. Let them come to the conclusion themselves to reinforce their self-esteem and build confidence.

5. *Ask them about it later.* Once you have helped them find a solution, always follow-up on how things went after they implemented the solution. Don't let it alone so soon - new developments always tend to hamper progress.

Don't

1. *(Don't) Try to fix it.* Being an adult and having experienced something similar in your childhood, it is natural to want to fix things for your child. But always keep in mind that if you do this job for them, you are taking away their chance to be an independent thinker. You want them to be brave and smart about handling their own affairs. Eventually, they will have to rely solely on their own judgement - so help them develop it while you can, and bestow as much problem-solving wisdom as you can.

2. *(Don't) Ask them to change.* Just because a problem is difficult to solve, doesn't mean we should get rid of it. Letting something go unsolved is not a solution - rather, it exacerbates the problem. Therefore, avoid suggesting something as drastic as this and let them work things out in their mind. You need to hold on to the trust you have as a parent, and if you become one of the other voices asking them to change - you risk losing that trust. Believe in them as they are.

3. *(Don't) Be biased.* While telling you what happened, your child may have represented themselves as the victim, and that won't always be the case.

Sometimes, they are the ones who started the drama and now want sympathy when their friends turned them down. So don't treat them like a victim if you know they are at fault. Instead, use this opportunity to show them the mirror and talk about the repercussions their actions had. Trust in their words, but try to ask the right questions to eke the truth out.

4. *(Don't) Allow bullying.* If you think that the actions of your child make them a bully towards other kids, don't hold back from pointing it out. Encourage them as you used to, to see things from the point of view of others. Use it as a lesson in empathy. Subtly remind them how they would have felt if they were at the receiving end of the bullying. Encourage them to apologize and make amends with those they have hurt and teach them that there is no shame in doing so. Bullying stunts the growth of not only your own child - but any other affected child. Don't allow it, and we can all grow together.

Chapter 5: Friendships at Home

Our very first relationships are with our parents. Our first memory is of them smiling at us with tears of joy in their eyes. We remember how they couldn't hold back their excitement when we took our first steps. We remember how proud they had been when we pronounced our first words. And then we made them even more proud by turning out to be well-behaved, obedient, and successful - most of the time. It may be true that we don't remember these experiences exactly, but our parents definitely do. And we surely remember these with our own kids.

Healthy relationships at home between parents and children is what lays the foundation of a happy home. Without a nourishing relationship it can feel like living in a home without walls. Our relationships provide the structure that keeps us safe. Households where parents are violent, emotionally or physically, risk injuring their own children in the same way. Patterns in parents may beget the same patterns in their children. And so be sure to set the right patterns with your children. Use this unconscious mimicry to your advantage and role model strong choices for your kids. The greater your role modelling, the greater your chances of your children discovering a happy and fulfilled life.

In this chapter, we will look at the role good and bad in-home relationships play on the upbringing of a child. And most importantly, we will investigate the age old question: Should I try to be a friend to my child?

The Need for Healthy Friendship Between Parents

Parents play an important role in the development of social skills in children. They are the ones who teach them to interact with others successfully. One of the most important qualities they teach children is how to build respectful relationships based on love, acceptance, and trust. And since the very first relationship children create is with their parents, how they view that relationship can say a lot about the kind of relationships they will seek in life. For instance, if a parent is highly critical and unloving, the child will assume that that's how relationships are supposed to be. So they will allow others to hurt them and they themselves will criticize others - because it has been normalized. Children who have been raised in homes where domestic violence was a norm, run a greater risk of repeating that cycle and reacting with the same anger and frustration towards their own partners. If you witness abuse between your parents - that behavior becomes normalized.

It is always wise to avoid fighting and conflict in the home. If an argument escalates, as they tend to do, more than anything you need to be sure that your child is not caught in the crossfire. It can be difficult to schedule a conflict, but you need to gather control of your emotions for the good of your child. If a child witnesses a conflict, do your best - together, if you can - to explain the cause and the solution to that conflict. Help them understand positive conflict resolution to try and normalize that behavior. It is very easy to lose the trust of a child through conflict, so be sure to control it where you can. That trust will be helpful later in the difficult teenage years.

Conflict at home always carries the risk of seeping into other areas of your child's life. As conflict breeds anxiety and uncertainty, your child may develop these traits. At school, these traits may come out during an exam, or an important academic moment, and potentially damage their advancement or progress. They may not be bullied at school, or study in an anxious classroom - but that conflict at home has now bled into their academics.

Children may also resort back to behaviors and habits they used to have when they were younger. For instance, if the child had a habit of wetting their bed or sleepwalking, conflict and an anxious household could trigger this again. They may also be scared easily, have poor sleep, and hide or stutter words.

It can be difficult to broach this subject with your child. Especially when it comes to personal issues, or big picture concerns they may not be ready to deal with yet. But if you don't communicate with your child, they may begin to blame themselves for what goes on in the house. This internal blame will not only affect their mental peace, but again, also reflect on their academics. They may isolate themselves, break up with their friends, or indulge in risky behaviors to overcome the guilt and confusion.

Teenagers are at a special risk to find other negative ways to deal with conflict in the home. They are more active, self-determined, and able to navigate the outside world. They also have a greater network of friends and acquaintances to reach out to - for better or for worse. Teenagers may skip school, get in trouble with the law, hurt others, or get involved in unsafe or unprotected activities. They may also bully others to feel good about themselves if they're upset, which only feeds the cycle of violence. It is more imperative than ever to communicate honestly with your children when they are teenagers to avoid these lashings out.

Statistical data suggests that in the United States, approximately 15 million children have witnessed at least one incidence of violence in their homes (McDonald et al., 2006). That is 15 million potential new cycles of violence. Of course, it is absolutely not a guarantee - and wrong to suggest a direct link - but may still increase the risk of violence later on in a child's life. When behavior is normalized, it runs this risk. According to another study, girls who have witnessed abuse at home by their father towards their mother are six times more likely to be abused than girls raised in non-abusive families (Monnat & Chandler, 2015). The same study also highlights that boys who have seen their fathers abuse their mothers are ten times more likely to abuse their partners. Abuse should never be tolerated in your household - point of fact.

Should I Be Friends With My Child?

Now that we have established the importance of healthy relationships and the impact any guiding relationship can leave on children, it brings us to the most pressing question: can a parent and child be friends? Or perhaps a better question would be - *should* a parent and child be friends?

A Parent as Friend

Some will argue that this school of thought is indeed the ideal way to parent. On paper, it can seem more casual, comforting, and less suffocating. Many believe that it allows their kids to be more expressive and honest with them, and thus prevent secrecy and dishonesty. Additionally, some believe that it brings them closer to their child, and promotes stability and harmony.

But this is not always the case. A significant flaw outweighs most of those benefits: too much freedom. Although it is healthy for your child to feel free in their actions, limitations aren't a strict negative. Limitations can often be constructive - and coming from a parent, often are. Without the moral guidelines, the role modelling, or the discipline, children can land themselves in hot water. When parents allow excess freedom to their kids, they may start to push the limits. They start to believe that they can get away with anything and don't always make the right choices. If this is the case, a "friendly" parent is not always able to push back or provide wise guidance. Their status has been diminished in the relationship, to just another member of the friend network.

A Parent as Parent

A similar criticism can indeed be levied against parents who restrict freedom *too* much, and who "parent" too heavily. This can be a stifling style of parenting that almost encourages rebellion. So there is a fine balance in this. But the need for a trusted source, a level of responsibility, and the odd bit of discipline often makes traditional parenting a more valued resource than "friendly" parenting.

Many believe that strict parenting is the best way to instill good values and morals. Without this strong guidance, they worry that children can grow wild and rebellious. The thought is that too much freedom is exploitable. Many also think that strict boundaries and parameters for acceptable and unacceptable behaviors speak for themselves, and there is no need to argue about them.

However, this isn't a perfect model either. Not allowing argument or constructive discussion about boundaries doesn't ensure that these rules will be followed. And heavy discipline upon breaking these rules doesn't ensure they will be understood.

Without proper reasoning, and an explanation for these boundaries, they can be misconstrued as suffocating. If the boundaries are there to help ensure the safety of your child - try to explain that to them. Help them understand why the fence was erected here, and what lies on the other side. Otherwise, the child is quite likely to vault the fence and find out on their own.

So, Where's the Middle Ground?

If it's not being their friend, and not a disciplinarian, then what is it? Where's the compromise between authority and leniency? How do we provide freedom within a structure, or boundaries within independence?. In order to establish peace and harmony, a strong approach to parenting is to become a mentor figure.

Being a mentor means you have an interest in your child's life, but don't dictate it. You can play with them, but don't become too fixated on doing things for them. You maintain some form of control over their activities but don't hover over them like a helicopter. You are soft but not too soft. You are strict but not too strict. You are there when they need you but not a complete pushover. Ideally, you should be ready to step in when they need you and be prepared to let them live when they don't.

The key is to not overstep at either of the roles. A mentor is together a coach, guide, and teacher. You can provide guidance, but let them solve their own problems. The hardest part is you have to step aside sometimes and let them be hurt - safely - so they can learn from the experience. In the same way, you have to let them enjoy their life, and love life, in order to learn from those positive experiences as well. You can share in these feelings too, and talk about them. When you feel scared, or anxious, check in with your child. But always stay a step behind them, so that if they fall, you can pick them up and tell them that everything will be alright.

Structure and Discipline

No matter what age, all children need some level of discipline and structure in their lives. Structure provides boundaries to test, and charts the world they can explore. Without discipline, they may act rashly, learn consequences another way, and suffer from anxiety and stress. Building strong social skills and giving them directions on how to lead a successful life is only possible when they see you as the one in control, and they respect your position. Having structure allows them to know what is expected of them and what to expect in return. When they have strong self-control, they feel comfortable facing challenges and grabbing opportunities. When a household is unpredictable and values are inconsistent, this structure is difficult to maintain. A mentor-figure parent needs to be able to balance their role in the house carefully to cultivate this environment.

Younger children aren't developmentally and emotionally able to know their boundaries. This can lead to poor decision making and blaming others for their mistakes. When parents are friends instead of a mentor, there is no strong hand to guide them in the right direction and help them cope with the challenges of growing up.

Rules and Boundaries

Some parents only have a single goal in mind when raising children: please them. Although a positive strategy, it doesn't prepare children for the real world when they go out and discover that life isn't a bed of roses. When parents intentionally decide against setting rules and regulations because they assume it would upset their child or stop them from achieving greatness, they are wrong. It really only leads to disappointment and failure.

The reason children need boundaries is that they will instinctively test their surroundings until they brush up against them. Watch a young child crawl - they will continue until they brush up against the edge of their world. Those boundaries need to be set safely so they can be found and understood before crawling into the riskier territory beyond. An interesting case is that too many or too few boundaries can both lead to insecurity and anxiety. Both cases stem from not understanding the environment properly. Without boundaries, the world can be too vast and overwhelming. With too strict boundaries - the world can become small and stifling.

Dependency

When a parent becomes a friend, rather than a mentor-figure, kids start to look up to them for everything. As a "friend," you always have the answers, but now you have become the answer for everything. It is always recommended to keep a healthy separation between the parent and the child. This separation prepares a child for their eventual independence. When parents become friends, and do everything together, it can become harder for the child to imagine a life without them. They may also fail to develop a strong personality and an identity of their own. As a result, they may forever stay in the nest and not function well as an adult. If they do move out and build a romantic relationship, they will have the same expectations from their partner as they had from their parents. That can be a hard role to fill, and unjust to the partner - leading to an imbalanced relationship.

Chapter 6: Fostering Healthy Bonds

Have there been days when you constantly fight with your child? Do you seem to have opposite opinions about everything, like what to order for dinner or what to wear to a family gathering? The disagreements always end, but they still leave behind negative energy – the type that overwhelms us from time to time. It can be hard to get past it and move one. Often, kids just want to be right. As they self-determine, they want to select the answers for once. They want to do things their way and not the way their parents expect them to. The difficulty as a parent is to let them be "right" once in a while, even if you know how it will end up. In your lived wisdom, you need to take a backseat to their youthful drive, and avoid the dangerous condescension that can come with good advice. Without this give-and-take, relationships can become sour. Every time there is a discussion, it ends with another argument and everything falls apart once again. If you have dealt with this behavior lately, you may be stuck in a power struggle.

In this chapter, we come to understand what power struggles are, their impact on the relationship between a parent and a child, and how parents can avoid them.

Power Struggles in Relationships

Imagine this: you told your teenage daughter to clean her room two days ago. It still is in the same condition – if not worse. If you have guests visiting today and are too busy to go upstairs and set it for them. You feel hurt that they didn't adhere to your request. It is difficult to turn this experience into a learning moment, as the consequences will mostly come back on you as the host.

On the other side, your daughter is holding a grudge against you because you grounded her over something you deemed insignificant, which really was everything to her. Her friends went to a party without her and now she is anxious to be excluded from her social circle. She blames you for purposely punishing her so that she would miss the party. She wants to get back at you and show you her independence through protest.

Now both of you are angry at each other, but not ready to talk it out. You two are just waiting for the other to give in and apologize. To make matters worse, you have guests over and have to perform as host for them, without being your real self with your daughter.

This is a power struggle. Power struggles can be about any and everything, no matter how big or small. They usually come with one distinct feature: an ultimatum. An ultimatum could be something as simple as demanding an apology. Ultimatums carry too much pressure, so just don't set them. If you stand by them, you risk dying on your sword for something that could be worked out in a much more effective way. Especially when coupled with negative thoughts, they can only breed discontent, and make things worse.

Power struggles, in any relationship, can be highly toxic. You may recognize them best in the workplace, when there is intense competition or status-shifting among employees. The same takes place inside a household. They are known to bring out the worst in everyone involved, and set roots of bitterness. With children, they often play out through public tantrums, manipulation, and self-doubt. They have an uncanny ability to play a parent against their public image - piercing the veil of social expectations. These reactions often lead to resentment, hatred, and prolonged suffering for both parties. They need to be dealt with from the beginning, stopping conflict from brewing before it begins.

How to Lead Without a Power Struggle

Another scenario to consider. Your child is taking all the time in the world to get dressed and get out of the door. You're already late for work and keep shouting their name to come out. In doing so, you get more frustrated, and they get the secret joy of rebellion. The morning is already ruined for both of you, and once in the car, you avoid talking to each other completely. A question is brought up, and your tone is filled with sarcasm and accusations. Your child reacts accordingly, and you find yourself in another power struggle. Below are some tips to deal with a tense situation effectively, ensuring that your parent-child relationship stays strong. Remember, sometimes you have to take a step back and lose a little ground, in order for a true parenting win.

1. *Let them have the last word. You might think this is odd and it may be difficult to do. However, it can benefit your relationship greatly. If your child says something negative, don't react. Don't stoke the fire. Be the role model and mentor you need to be, and let it go. Model the behavior you hope to see in them. Set your dignity aside for just a moment. You'll get it back soon - you're the provider and they depend on you. They know this, but a moment can get heated. Once your child lets an insult out of their system and fails to see a charged response, they will cut it out themselves. But set your own boundaries - when enough's enough - you let them know.*

2. *Validate their feelings. When you are in the middle of a power struggle with your child, let them pour their heart out. Listen with compassion without interrupting them. Once they are done, let them know that you have heard them*

loud and clear, and that you understand why they feel that way. When a child feels listened to and validated, it helps them be more expressive and calm the next time around. The world can seem like it ignores them sometimes, so don't ignore them as well.

3. *Give them a reason. Often, children disobey and start a power struggle because they don't have a compelling reason to obey you. They must know why they should do as they are told, and what the consequences are - positive or negative. Give them a choice and let them pick their own consequences. For example, "if you get ready sooner, we will have more time together, more time with your friends, and we will be at each other's throats much less."*

4. *Offer a choice. This is another way of letting them decide for themselves. If the power struggle is happening over homework and the kid tells you how much they hate you when you make them do it, offer them a constructive choice. Again, the world doesn't offer them much choice generally - so give them a bit of agency here in the household to make their own decisions.*

5. *Reframe their imagination.* Another tip that works well is a reframing strategy. If

your child can't stand still for very long when asked - reframe the question. Ask them to play a soldier, or a different non-military role, and watch them snap to attention. If parents reframe orders in ways that interest children, power struggles can be avoided.

6. *Build your relationship early. The best way to prevent power struggles is by knowing your child's interests and spending time with them to develop these. If you share interests, the rebellion phase will be less natural. This also serves as a great time to bond. Consider it an investment in their later years. When they turn 25, they will thank you for your investment. That's a long time coming, but it will set them up for life - trust in that.*

7. *Be compassionate.* Role model the behaviors you wish to see. Say your own please and thank yous. A child will mimic the role models in their life through instinct. Add to that a kind and warm tone and you are already halfway there. Kids of any age want love and attention. When they feel valued, they are more likely to follow through.

8. *Ignore unnecessary chatter. Again, you can't be reacting over everything they say. Pick battles worth fighting and*

ignore the rest. Some habits get parents all worked up. But kids are kids - they are young and impulsive. For example, you may feel annoyed by the way they tap their foot on the ground when doing something. Correct them, but try to understand why they tap. Are they nervous, anxious, or energized? Try to focus on solving the bigger problems, not just the symptoms.

9. *Be considerate. If they don't feel like finishing their vegetables today but have been doing so excellently for the past week, give them the day off. Be a kind and merciful leader. Be flexible so they know that you can be understanding. Your kids need to see that quality in you, or you run the risk of them not confiding in you when they should.*

10. *Use the pivot strategy. Pivot is the art of redirection. Similar to reframing imagination. Pivoting is saying yes instead of no, and still solving the problem. For example, "No, we can't go out before you take a shower". This seems rather negative. Try to rephrase that no into a yes that works for you: "Yes, we will go out - once you have taken your bath". You are saying the same thing, but in a different tone.*

Chapter 7: Friendship FAQs

In this final chapter, we tackle some of the most frequently asked questions many parents have when teaching their children social skills and the art of making friends. These questions appear most frequently on social platforms and online parenting forums.

My child doesn't have any friends, should I worry?

We associate friendship with happiness. We think that if our child has lots of friends, it means they are happy. But this isn't always the case. Many kids have a close group of friends and just do fine with them. Some kids only have a single best friend and don't seem to need anyone else. Children all show affection for others in different ways.

It is completely normal for your child to have a few close friends and not an entire army. In fact, the bonds might even be stronger between a select few. But if you are worried that they have no strong friends, then consider your options.

Find out what stands in their way. Are they shy? Do they have specific and unshared interests? Look for the obstacles in their way. As the parent, you know them best, but don't be afraid to ask them.

If they are afraid of rejection, help make some introductions. Or go out of your way to befriend other parents, and bring the children together that way. A dinner party is a small sacrifice to make for the children. But don't force these relationships - they need to develop naturally.

Remind your child that every other child is in the same position. Everyone is scared and nervous, and everyone wants to make a friend. Encourage them to reach out.

Role model the ideal friendships in your own life. Invite your friends around so your children can see these ideas normalized and pick up on patterns of socialization. Be supportive, kind, outgoing, and compassionate towards your friends and hope that your child picks up these values too.

My child is always taken advantage of by their friends. What can I do?

Sometimes life is unfair, and especially to children. The innocents always get hurt the most. As a parent, nothing hurts more than to see a child being treated unfairly and left to suffer alone.

However, as tempting as it seems, you can't be too forceful in ending a bad relationship. Instead, provide guidance, and let them learn from their mistakes. But be ready to catch them when they fall. Consider bringing up in conversation a past friendship in your own life that turned into a toxic relationship. Emphasize how you saw the signs, and how you acted. Be subtle, and turn on your acting charm - but be honest. Again, role model the behaviors you wish your child to adopt.

We have just moved houses and my child doesn't have any friends in this area. How do I encourage him to make new ones?

Introductions are a lot harder in a new place. But be patient. Kids need time to adjust to a new place. This is a lot of information to take in, a lot of anxiety, and they may be hesitant to take on more anxiety in the form of a fragile new friendship.

Just do what you can to keep the options in front of them. Set up playdates or get them involved in school clubs. Invite their study partners over. Even explore the city or neighborhood with them. Give them experiences that make them confident, and confidence will spill over into relationships.

How do I make my child do things without throwing a tantrum or power struggle?

There are certainly days when everything can set a child off. Instead of reacting to their tantrums, act friendly and empathetic. Be their mentor and guide them through their emotions. They must know that you are on their side. Discover what's going on inside - it is almost a guarantee it isn't about whatever "little thing" sets them off (it's never just a little thing).

Just talk to them about it. Be ready to listen. Ask the right questions. Explain your point of view, and why certain tasks need to be completed. Tell them your own feelings - but don't get too heavy. Adults deal with a lot more than a child can handle sometimes.

Simplify your feelings - whether sad, tired, hungry, or sleepy.

This can be an effective way to prevent power struggles because they view you as a concerned parent who genuinely cares and wants to make things better for you. Grow empathy in your household.

Am I in the wrong to fix their problems so they don't feel hurt anymore?

Unfortunately, sometimes you will be in the wrong here. Fixing problems all the time for your child can lead to dependency. Children must be prepared to handle their own problems when they can. You may have the answers, and seeing them go through that negative phase can make your heart ache. But this is how we learn and become self-reliant. Take a single step back - far enough they can discover on their own, but not too far so that you're out of reach.

Encourage wise decision-making with roleplaying. Introduce to them games and activities that improve their cognitive thinking and problem-solving skills. Games like puzzles, riddles, strategy games, and math problems can develop these skills.

My child doesn't share things with me. What should I do?

Many kids, especially teenagers, keep their personal life private. As they grow older, they tend to confide more often in their new social circles, rather than their parents. Depending on your parenting style, they may also be worried about the resulting discipline - or equally important, a lack of discipline, which can be read as a lack of caring.

There are many ways to prevent secrecy, which typically involve growing communication skills. Discuss your daily routines. Be an active listener. Confide in them yourself - but not too much. Remember, adult lives are often too complex for a child to pick up on right now. Emphasize why trust is important, and what dangers lie beyond if that trust is broken. Encourage conversations on subjects that interest them - feign interest if you have to, but always be honest.

Conclusion

Strong friendships are an essential part of a child's life. Friends bring joy and happy expectations about the world. Friends see the best in us and love us for the worst. Friends motivate us to push all limits and set new benchmarks.

Not having such an important figure to rely on early in life can be detrimental. It deprives kids of that joy and love. It prevents them from learning many crucial social skills which are an important asset in life. And importantly, it isolates children with personal problems and no external support system.

This book offered a guide to emphasize the importance of good friends in life, but we also looked at ways that you, as a parent, can play a role. Your role in many cases may simply be to take a step back. It may be to brush up on your own social skills, or take a look at your own actions. Regardless of what actions need to be taken to improve your child's environment, simply acknowledging them is the first step. Weigh your options, and set a course of action.

An important thought we want you to take away from this guide is that it doesn't matter as much if your child is the most popular kid in school, or the one that sits alone at lunch. If your child is happy, then that is something to celebrate. Continue to encourage positive experiences. And if your child is unhappy, then the time for action is now. Remember your guiding role as parent, and be there to listen to whatever your child needs. That's it - that's the core principle. If you can just do that, then you are indeed the best example of being a caring and devoted parent. You've got this.

Thank you for giving this book a read. I hope you loved reading it as much as I enjoyed writing it. It would make me the happiest person on earth if you would take a moment to leave an honest review. All you have to do is visit the site where you purchased this book: It's that simple! The review doesn't have to be a full-fledged paragraph; a few words will do. Your few words will help others decide if this is what they should be reading as well. Thank you in advance, and best of luck with your parenting adventures. Every moment is a joyous one with a child.

References

7 Simple Strategies to Avoid Power Struggles. (2014, October 15). https://www.psychologytoday.com/intl/blog/what-great-parents-do/201410/7-simple-strategies-avoid-power-struggles

13 Ways to Avoid Power Struggles. (2018, July 17). https://www.thepathway2success.com/13-ways-to-avoid-power-struggles/

Derhally, L. A. (2016, July 25). The importance of childhood friendships, and how to nurture them. https://www.washingtonpost.com/news/parenting/wp/2016/07/25/the-importance-of-childhood-friendships-and-how-to-nurture-them/

DeScioli, P., & Kurzban, R. (2009). The alliance hypothesis for human friendship. PLoS ONE.

Dickson, D. J., Huey, M., Laursen, B., Kiuru, N., & Nurmi, J.-E. (2018). Parent contributions to friendship stability during the primary school years. Journal of Family Psychology, 32(2), 217–228.

Essential Friendship Skills for Kids. (n.d.). https://www.counselorkeri.com/2019/06/17/teach-kids-friendship-skills/

Ferrer, M., & Fugate, A. (n.d.). The Importance of Friendship for School-Age Children. IFAS Extension.

Fletcher, J., Ross, S., & Zhang, Y. (2013). The Consequences of Friendships: Evidence on the Effect of Social Relationships in School on Academic Achievement.

Goldman, J. G. (2013, January 24). How and why do we pick our friends? https://www.bbc.com/future/article/201301 23-what-are-friends-really-for

Improve Skills in Maintaining and Strengthening Friendship Bonds between Kids. (2014, January 1). https://www.lifeway.com/en/articles/parenti ng-family-six-building-blocks-for-friendship

Jones, D. E., Greenberg, M., & Crowley, M. (2015). Early Social-Emotional Functioning and Public Health: The Relationship Between Kindergarten Social Competence and Future Wellness. American Journal of Public Health, 2283_2290.

Lewis, C. S. (1960). The beloved works of C.S. Lewis. New York: HarperCollins Publishers.

McDonald, R., Jouriles, E. N., Ramisetty-Mikler, S., Caetano, R., & Green, C. E. (2006). Estimating the number of American children living in partner-violent families. Journal of Family Psychology, 137-142.

Monnat, S. M., & Chandler, R. F. (2015). Long Term Physical Health Consequences of Adverse Childhood Experiences. The Sociological quarterly, 723–752.

Mourier, J., Vercelloni, J., & Planes, S. (2012). Evidence of social communities in a spatially structured network of a free-ranging shark species. Animal Behaviour, 389-401.

Oakley, J. (2019, September 21). The Risks And Benefits Of Being Your Child's Friend (And Where To Draw The Line). https://www.yourtango.com/2019326645/parenting-advice-should-friend-your-child

Plato. (2013). Works Of Plato: the trial and death of socrates (Vol. III). New York: Cosimo Classics.

Schwartz, P. (n.d.). Child Behavior: The importance of friendship. https://hvparent.com/importance-of-friendship

Schwarz, N. (2016, February 23). Your Child's Friendship Drama: Do's and Don'ts for Parents. https://imperfectfamilies.com/your-childs-friendship-drama-dos-and-donts-for-parents/

Should You Be Your Child's Best Friend? (2019, September 19). https://kidskingdom.ca/kanata/disciplinarian-or-best-friend-your-role-as-a-parent/

What is a Power Struggle? (2017, February 27).https://philosophicaltherapist.com/2017/02/27/what-is-a-power-struggle/

www.ingramcontent.com/pod-product-compliance
Lightning Source LLC
Chambersburg PA
CBHW062042080426
42734CB00012B/2534